The World and Its People
COMMUNITIES AND RESOURCES

The World and Its People

SERIES AUTHORS

Val E. Arnsdorf, Professor,
  College of Education, University of Delaware,
  Newark, Delaware

Carolyn S. Brown, Late Principal,
  Robertson Academy School, Nashville, Tennessee

Kenneth S. Cooper, Professor of History, Emeritus,
  George Peabody College for Teachers, Vanderbilt
  University, Nashville, Tennessee

Alvis T. Harthern, Professor of Education,
  University of Montevallo, Montevallo, Alabama

Timothy M. Helmus, Classroom Teacher,
  City Middle and High School, Grand Rapids,
  Michigan

Bobbie P. Hyder, Elementary Education Coordinator,
  Madison County School System, Huntsville,
  Alabama

Theodore Kaltsounis, Professor and Associate Dean,
  College of Education, University of Washington,
  Seattle, Washington

Richard H. Loftin, Director of Curriculum and Staff
  Development,
  Aldine Independent School District, Houston, Texas

Norman J.G. Pounds, Former University Professor of
  Geography,
  Indiana University, Bloomington, Indiana

Edgar A. Toppin, Professor of History and Dean of the
  Graduate School,
  Virginia State University, Petersburg, Virginia

GRADE–LEVEL CONTRIBUTORS

Paula Allaert, Teacher,
  St. Therese School, Portland, Oregon

Carol Armour, Teacher,
  Marie V. Duffy Elementary School, Wharton, New Jersey

Ellen Gremillion, Teacher,
  Parkview Elementary School, Baton Rouge, Louisiana

Geoffrey Kashdan, Principal,
  New Jersey Regional Day School at Morris for Handicapped
    Children, Morristown, New Jersey

Carolyn Lombardo, Teacher,
  Ferrara Elementary School, East Haven, Connecticut

Map Chapter by Stan Christodlous, Executive Editor, Social Studies,
Silver Burdett Company

COMMUNITIES AND RESOURCES

RICHARD H. LOFTIN   Director of Curriculum and Staff Development
Aldine Independent School District, Houston, Texas

SILVER BURDETT COMPANY Morristown, New Jersey
Glenview, Ill • San Carlos, Calif. • Dallas • Atlanta
Agincourt, Ontario

ISBN 0-382-02831-7

CONTENTS

UNIT **1** Learning About Communities   *1*

CHAPTER I   *Using Maps, Graphs, and Time Lines*   *2*
The Earth • Maps • Scale • Communities
and States • Our Country • Continents and
Hemispheres • Latitude and Longitude •
Time Lines • Graphs

        CHAPTER REVIEW   •   SKILLS DEVELOPMENT   *34—35*

CHAPTER 2   *Studying Your Community*   *36*
Using Maps • Learning About the Past •
Working in a Community • The Seeing Eye—
A Very Special Place • Having Fun in a
Community

        CHAPTER REVIEW   •   SKILLS DEVELOPMENT   *64—65*

UNIT **2** Living in Different Communities   *67*

CHAPTER 3   *Living in Cities*   *68*
Cities Have a Past • People Live and Work in
Cities • People Have Fun in Cities • Cities
Need Transportation

        CHAPTER REVIEW   •   SKILLS DEVELOPMENT   *94—95*

CHAPTER 4   *Living in Smaller Communities*   *96*
People Live and Work in a Small Town •
Community Events • People Have Fun in
Towns • Transportation from the Suburbs
to the City

        CHAPTER REVIEW   •   SKILLS DEVELOPMENT   *116—117*

UNIT 3 Farms and Resources Support Our Communities
119

CHAPTER 5 *Farms and Ranches Support Our Communities* **120**
Farms Long Ago and Now • A Dairy Farm •
A Vegetable Farm • A Wheat Farm • A Citrus
Farm • Ranching • A Livestock Show and
Rodeo

CHAPTER REVIEW • SKILLS DEVELOPMENT **140—141**

CHAPTER 6 *Natural Resources Support Our Communities* **142**
A Coal-Mining Community • An Oil-Drilling
Community • Oil from the Ground to You •
Fishing Communities • Conserving Our
Natural Resources

CHAPTER REVIEW • SKILLS DEVELOPMENT **160—161**

UNIT 4 Citizenship in the United States
163

CHAPTER 7 *We Need Rules* **164**
Communities Make and Keep Rules •
Communities Provide Services • Washington,
D.C.—Our Capital City

CHAPTER REVIEW • SKILLS DEVELOPMENT **184—185**

CHAPTER 8 *Bringing Our People Together* **186**
Telephone, Radio, and Television •
Newspapers, Magazines, and Books • Letters

CHAPTER REVIEW • SKILLS DEVELOPMENT **203—204**

ATLAS **206**
GRAPH APPENDIX **217**
GAZETTEER **226**
GLOSSARY **231**
REFERENCE TABLE: Area And Population Of The Fifty States **239**
INDEX **240**

MAPS

Directions — 4
From Photograph to Map — 7
A School — 11
A Community — 13
South Carolina — 14
The United States of America — 16-17
North America — 18
The Earth's Continents — 19
The Western Hemisphere — 21
The Eastern Hemisphere — 21
The Southern Hemisphere — 21
The Northern Hemisphere — 21
Latitude Lines — 22
Longitude Lines — 22
Putting Latitude and Longitude Together — 24

Using Latitude and Longitude — 26-27
The United States — 39
New Jersey — 40
Morris County — 41
Morristown and Morris Township — 41
Valley of Mexico — 70
Washington Metropolitan Area Transit System — 92
A Neighborhood — 117
The United States: Coalfields — 145
The United States: Oil Fields — 149
Washington, D.C. — 182-183
The United States: Postal ZIP Code Regions — 199
Texas: Postal ZIP Code Areas — 200

ATLAS

The World — 206-207
The United States of America — 208-209
North America — 210
South America — 211

Eurasia — 212-213
Europe — 214
Africa — 215
Australia and New Zealand — 216

GRAPHS

Introducing Pictographs
United States Population: 1790-1830 — 30
Introducing Pie Graphs
United States Population in 1790 — 31
Introducing Bar Graphs
United States Population: 1790-1830 — 32

Introducing Line Graphs
United States Population: 1790-1830 — 33
Leading Dairy Cattle States — 123
People Living on Farms in the United States — 141
Size of Farms in the United States — 141

GRAPH APPENDIX

The Earth: Land and Water — 217
The Earth: Land Area by Continents — 217
The Earth: Land Area by Countries — 217
The United States: Land Area by States — 217
The World: Largest Countries in Area — 218
The United States: Largest States in Area — 218

The World: Largest Islands in Area — 218
The United States: Largest Islands in Area — 218
The World: Longest Rivers — 219
The United States: Longest Rivers — 219
The World: Largest Lakes in Area — 219
The United States: Largest Lakes in Area — 219

The World: Leading Producers of Oil 220

The United States: Leading Producers of Oil 220

The World: Leading Producers of Coal 220

The United States: Leading Producers of Coal 220

The World: Leading Producers of Wheat 221

The United States: Leading Producers of Wheat 221

The World: Leading Producers of Fish 221

The United States: Leading Producers of Fish 221

Average Monthly Temperatures: San Francisco, California 222

Average Monthly Precipitation: San Francisco, California 222

Average Monthly Temperatures: Washington, D.C. 222

Average Monthly Precipitation: Washington, D.C. 222

Average Monthly Temperatures: Miami, Florida 223

Average Monthly Precipitation: Miami, Florida 223

Average Monthly Temperatures: Chicago, Illinois 223

Average Monthly Precipitation: Chicago, Illinois 223

Average Monthly Temperatures: New York, New York 224

Average Monthly Precipitation: New York, New York 224

Average Monthly Temperatures: Houston, Texas 224

Average Monthly Precipitation: Houston, Texas 224

Average Monthly Temperatures: Mexico City, Mexico 225

Average Monthly Precipitation: Mexico City, Mexico 225

Average Monthly Temperatures: San Juan, Puerto Rico 225

Average Monthly Precipitation: San Juan, Puerto Rico 225

DIAGRAMS, TIME LINES, AND TABLES

Four Main Directions 5

Using Scale 9

Time Line: Life of a Child 28

Time Line: Some Important Events in United States History 29

Table: United States Population: 1790–1830 29

Table: Businesses in the Morristown Area 50

An Automobile Assembly Line 78–79

A Baseball Schedule 95

A Ranch Today 136

A Coal-Mining Shaft 146

A Fish Ladder 159

A Mileage Chart 185

Time Line: Some Important Events in Communications 188

A Communications Satellite 190

Table: Area and Population of the Fifty States 239

END-OF-CHAPTER SKILLS DEVELOPMENT

Using the Atlas and the Gazetteer 35

Finding the Main Idea in a Paragraph 65

Reading a Schedule 95

Reading a Map 117

Reading Pictographs 141

Using an Index 161

Reading a Mileage Chart 185

Writing a Letter 204

Dear Student,

I am writing to you from my home in Humble, Texas. Before you begin your work in social studies, I want to tell you a little about myself. I also want to tell you about some of the subjects you will be studying in this book.

Like many of you, I no longer live in the place where I was born. I was born in a small town—Alexandria, Louisiana. I grew up and went to school in a larger town—Baton Rouge, Louisiana. Later I moved to a large city—Houston, Texas. This is where I work today. I live in a smaller town not far from Houston. The community is named Humble. You will learn more about Humble in Chapter 4.

As you can see, I have lived in several different communities. In this book I want to share with you some of the things I have learned about communities. You will read about a number of communities throughout the United States. In some ways, these cities and towns will be like your community and mine. In other ways, these places will be different from your community and mine. You will learn about these similarities and differences.

You will also learn about the earth's natural resources. Resources help us in many ways. Our homes and furniture may be made of wood. Wood comes from trees, a valuable natural resource. Our homes may be heated with coal, oil, or natural gas, other valuable resources. Our cars and trucks and most other means of transportation need gasoline to run. Gasoline is made from oil. The soil and the seas are valuable resources that give us food. These and many other natural resources are important in our daily lives. You will learn more about how we use resources and why it is important that we use our resources wisely.

I hope you will enjoy reading this book and learning about communities and resources.

Sincerely,

Richard Loftin

Learning About Communities

1 Using Maps, Graphs, and Time Lines

The Earth

VOCABULARY

globe	south
North Pole	east
north	west
South Pole	

Shape of the earth   This year you will learn about many places on the earth. Some are in our country. Some are in other parts of the world.

There are many ways of learning about the earth. One way is to look at it. Look out of the window now. How much of the earth can you see? Unless your school is on top of a mountain, you probably cannot see very much of the earth. If you were way out in space, you could see much more of the earth. But even then, you would see only about half the earth at one time. Do you know why that is true? The answer has to do with the earth's shape. You know the earth is like a ball. Look at a ball now. Notice that you can see only half the ball at one time.

Models   Have you ever played with miniature racing cars or toy trucks? Do you have any dolls? All of these are models of real things. They are made to look like real things. The important difference is that these models are smaller. The model airplane in the photograph at the top of page 3 is made to look just like the real airplane shown below it.

An important model is the **globe**. (Words in heavy type are in the Glossary that starts on page 231.) The globe is a model of the earth. The picture at the bottom left shows the earth from space. The globe at the bottom right shows the same half of the earth.

The toy airplane is a model of the real airplane. The globe is a model of the real earth.

2

DIRECTIONS

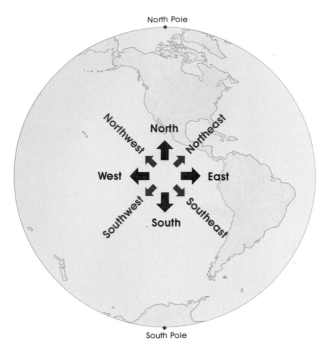

North is the direction toward the North Pole.

Direction One of the many things we can learn from a globe is direction. Look at the picture of the globe shown on this page. Find the **North Pole.** The North Pole is a very special place. It is the most northern place on the earth. **North** is the direction toward the North Pole. Find the **South Pole.** It too is a very special place. It is the most southern place on the earth. **South** is the direction toward the South Pole. North and south are opposite each other.

North and south are two directions. Two other directions are **east** and **west.** If you face north, east will be to your right. West will be to your left. East and west are opposite each other. North, south, east, and west are the four main directions. They help us understand where places are.

Look at the picture of the globe. Suppose you wanted to locate a place somewhere between the north arrow and the east arrow. You could say that the place is between the directions north and east. An easier way is to say that the place is in the northeast. What direction is between east and south? Between south and west? Between west and north? The four in-between directions—northeast, southeast, southwest, and northwest—also help us to understand where places are.

CHECKUP

1. What shape does the earth have?
2. What is a model of the earth called?
3. What are the four main directions?

4

If you face north, east is to your right.

Naomi Uemura of Japan made a trip alone to the North Pole. To celebrate reaching the North Pole, he shows flags of the countries that helped him make his trip.

5

The map shows the same area you see in the photograph.

Maps

Maps with symbols The globe is one tool that helps us learn more about the earth. But it is not the only tool we can use to learn about the earth. Another tool is a **map.** Maps, like globes, show us what the earth looks like. There are many different kinds of maps.

Most maps show what the earth looks like from directly overhead. The photograph on this page was taken from an airplane. Now look at the map on page 7. The map shows the same area as the photograph. Find some unusual shapes in the photograph. Then find those same shapes on the map.

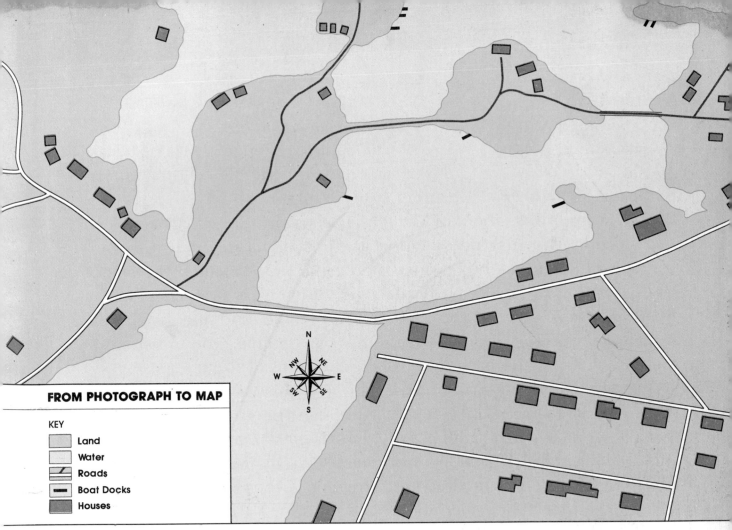

FROM PHOTOGRAPH TO MAP

KEY

Land
Water
Roads
Boat Docks
Houses

Notice that the map has a special part called the **key.** Most maps have keys. A key shows the **symbols** used on a map. The symbols stand for real things and places. Always look at the key to find out what real places and things the symbols stand for.

Find the drawing to the right of the map key. It is called a **compass rose.** Sometimes people call it a direction finder. The letters, N, E, S, and W stand for the directions north, east, south, and west. Can you guess what the letters NE, SE, SW, and NW stand for? If not, look back at the picture of the globe shown on page 4.

CHECKUP

1. Name two tools that help us learn more about the earth.
2. What do the symbols stand for in the map on page 7?
3. Where should you look to find what a symbol stands for?

Scale

┌─VOCABULARY────────────┐
│ scale   │
└───────────────────────┘

Scale on drawings   In order to show the correct size of places, maps are drawn to **scale.** Before we talk about scale on a map, let us see how scale is used in drawings. Look at the two drawings of a railroad train engine. Each engine is drawn to a different scale. The first one is drawn to a scale of 1 inch to 10 feet. This means that 1 inch on the drawing stands for 10 feet on the real train engine. The drawing is 6 inches long. Since each inch stands for 10 feet, you have to add six groups of 10 to find out how long the real engine is. It is 60 feet long (10 + 10 + 10 + 10 + 10 + 10 = 60).

The second drawing is smaller, so the scale is different. On this drawing, 1 inch stands for 20 feet. The drawing is 3 inches long. This time to find the length of the real engine, you must add three groups of 20 (20 + 20 + 20 = 60). The answer is still 60 feet. Although the scale has changed, the size of the real engine stays the same. No matter what size the drawing is, the size of the object is the same.

Many people enjoy model trains as a hobby. This model train is built to a scale of 1 to 148.

Although the scale of each drawing is different, the size of the train engine is the same.

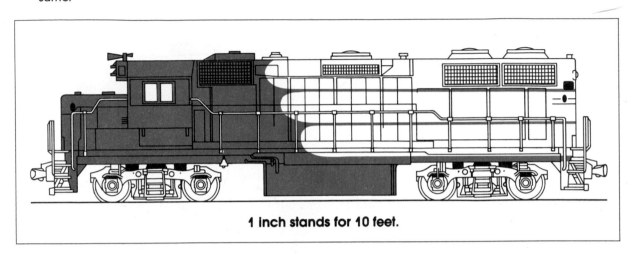

1 inch stands for 10 feet.

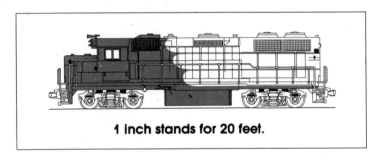

1 inch stands for 20 feet.

Scale on maps Now let us see how scale is used on a map. On the opposite page is a map of a school. A map cannot be drawn as big as the real size of the school. The map has to be smaller than the school. Look at the key on the map. Now find the numbered line. It is called a scale. The scale helps you find out how big a place is. It also helps you find how far one place is from another.

A library and a gymnasium (jim nā' zē əm) are found in many schools. Sometimes a gymnasium is part of an all-purpose room. Find these places on the map on page 11.

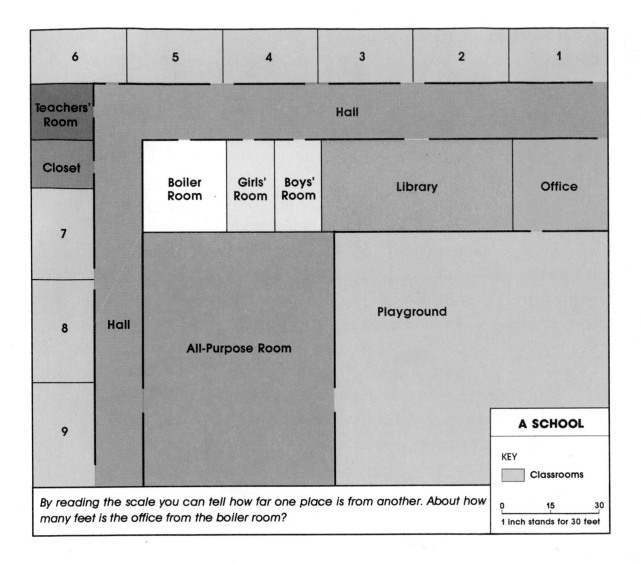

| 6 | 5 | 4 | 3 | 2 | 1 |

Teachers' Room	Hall
Closet	Boiler Room	Girls' Room	Boys' Room	Library	Office
7				
8	Hall	All-Purpose Room	Playground
9			

A SCHOOL

KEY

Classrooms

0   15   30
1 inch stands for 30 feet

By reading the scale you can tell how far one place is from another. About how many feet is the office from the boiler room?

The scale on the map above tells you that each inch on the map stands for 30 feet in the real school. We say that the map has a scale of 1 inch to 30 feet. Use your ruler to find out how long the school is on the map. It is 6 inches long. Since each inch stands for 30 feet, you have to add six groups of 30. The real school is 180 feet long (30 + 30 + 30 + 30 + 30 + 30 = 180).

CHECKUP

1. What does a map scale tell you?
2. Why can't a map be drawn to the full size of the place it shows?

Communities and States

Communities In the last section, you used a map of a school. Every school is part of a **community.** A community is a place in which people live, work, and play.

There are communities in many different places. Some are near **rivers.** A river is a body of water moving toward a **sea** or a **lake.** A sea is a very large body of salt water. The community shown on the map on page 13 has a lake next to it. A lake is a body of fresh water that has land all around it. Find the lake. What is its name? In the lake is a body of land with water all around it. We call such a body of land an **island.** This map also shows **mountains.** A mountain is land that rises high above the land around it. Look at the key to find the symbol for mountains.

Communities have homes, stores, places of worship, and other buildings. Cities and towns are communities. Cities are larger than towns. What is the name of your community? Is it a city? Is it a town? Can you name some cities and towns near you?

A school is an important building in a community.

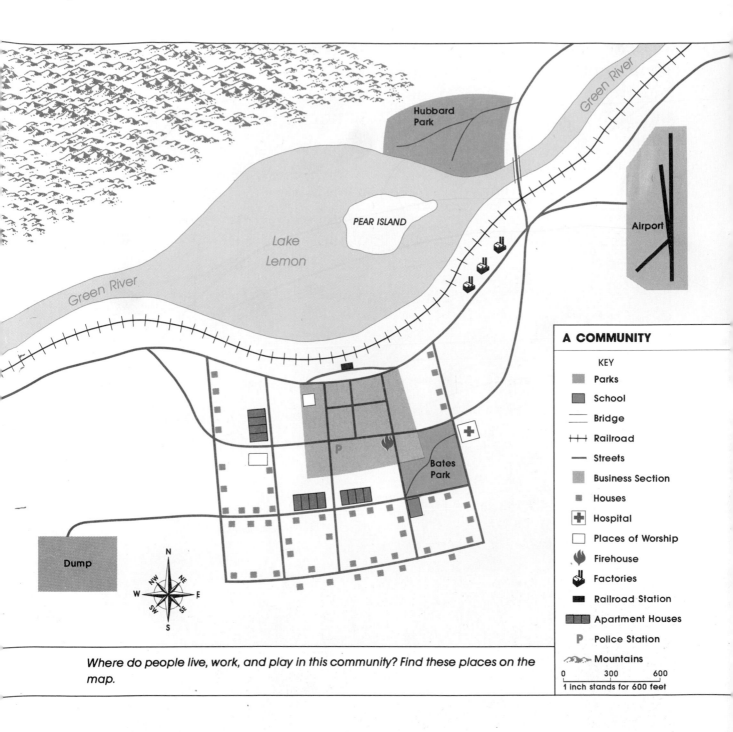

Where do people live, work, and play in this community? Find these places on the map.

A COMMUNITY

KEY

	Parks
	School
	Bridge
+++	Railroad
—	Streets
	Business Section
▪	Houses
+	Hospital
☐	Places of Worship
	Firehouse
	Factories
	Railroad Station
	Apartment Houses
P	Police Station
	Mountains

0   300   600
1 inch stands for 600 feet

States There are many communities in a **state.** A state is much larger than a town or a city. What is the name of your state?

Every state has a special city in which the state leaders make laws and plans for the whole state. This city is called the state **capital.** Do you know the capital of your state?

CHECKUP

1. Which is larger, a town or a city?
2. What is a state capital?

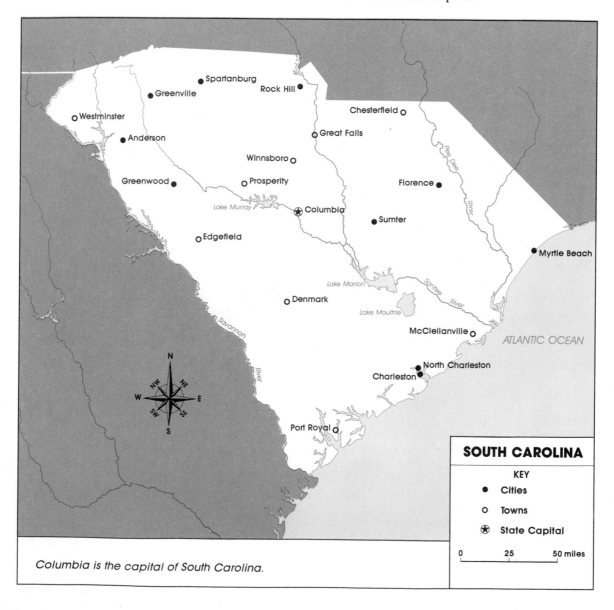

Columbia is the capital of South Carolina.

SOUTH CAROLINA

KEY
- ● Cities
- ○ Towns
- ✪ State Capital

0   25   50 miles

Our Country

Sizes of states Your state is only one of 50 states in our country. Some states are large. Alaska, Texas, and California are our three largest states. Some states are small. Rhode Island, Delaware, and Connecticut are our three smallest states. Find these six states on the map on pages 16−17. Put your finger on your state. What size is it?

People Some states have many people. California has more people than any other state. Some states have few people. Alaska has the fewest.

Physical features A **physical** (fiz′ ə kəl) **feature** is a part of the earth. Rivers, lakes, seas, and mountains are physical features. Most of Florida is a **peninsula.** That is, it has water almost all the way around it. Parts of other states are peninsulas.

There are islands in the rivers and lakes of many states. There are also islands in the ocean. One state, Hawaii, is made up entirely of islands. Hawaii is located in the Pacific Ocean.

Some states, like Colorado, have high mountains. One large part of our country is very flat. For miles and miles, all you can see is flat grasslands. This land is called the Great Plains. Nebraska is one state in the Great Plains.

Many states **border** on, or touch, the Atlantic Ocean. New Jersey and South Carolina are two states. Name the other states that touch the Atlantic Ocean.

One state that borders on the Pacific Ocean is California. It has a long **coastline.** What other states border on the Pacific? One of our largest states borders on the Arctic Ocean. This is our northernmost state, Alaska.

CHECKUP

1. How many states are there in the United States?
2. Which state is one of the largest in size but has the smallest number of people?
3. Which state is a peninsula?
4. Which state is a group of islands in the Pacific Ocean?

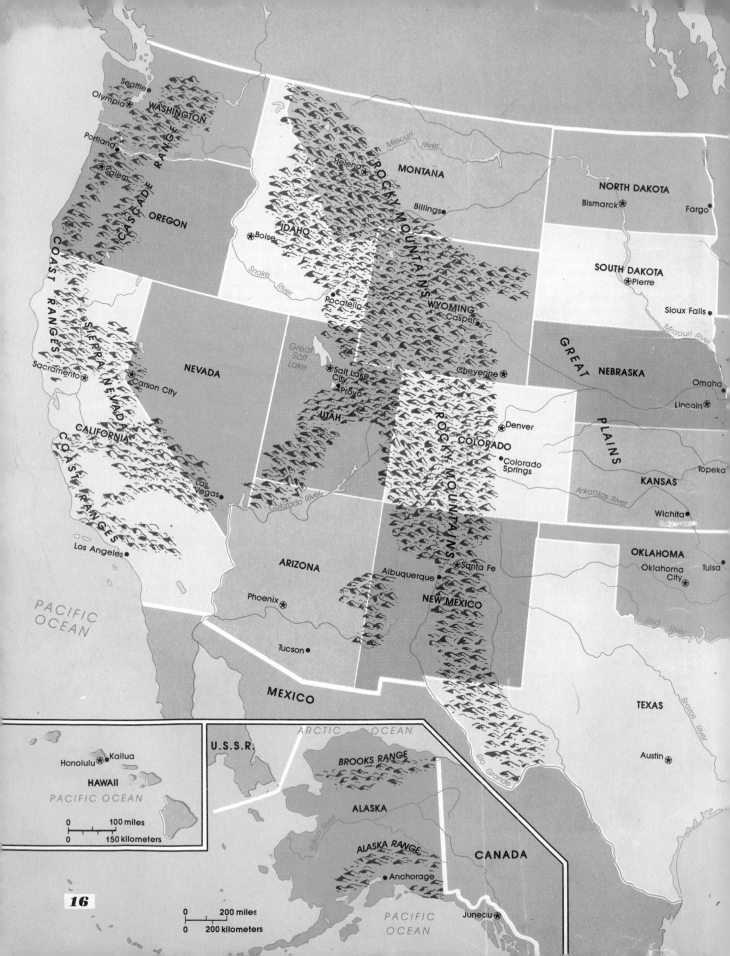

Seattle
Olympia
WASHINGTON
Portland
Salem
OREGON
CASCADE RANGE
COAST RANGES
SIERRA NEVADA
Sacramento
Carson City
NEVADA
CALIFORNIA
COAST RANGES
Las Vegas
Los Angeles
PACIFIC OCEAN
Phoenix
ARIZONA
Tucson

MEXICO

Columbia River
Snake River
Boise
IDAHO
Pocatello
Great Salt Lake
Salt Lake City
Provo
UTAH
Colorado River

Helena
MONTANA
Billings
ROCKY MOUNTAINS
WYOMING
Casper
Cheyenne
Denver
COLORADO
Colorado Springs
ROCKY MOUNTAINS
Albuquerque
Santa Fe
NEW MEXICO

Missouri River
NORTH DAKOTA
Bismarck
Fargo

SOUTH DAKOTA
Pierre
Sioux Falls
Missouri River
GREAT
NEBRASKA
Omaha
Lincoln
PLAINS
Topeka
KANSAS
Arkansas River
Wichita
OKLAHOMA
Oklahoma City
Tulsa
Red River

TEXAS
Austin
Rio Grande
Brazos River

ARCTIC OCEAN
U.S.S.R.
BROOKS RANGE
ALASKA
Yukon River
ALASKA RANGE
Anchorage
CANADA
Juneau
PACIFIC OCEAN

Honolulu
Kailua
HAWAII
PACIFIC OCEAN
0   100 miles
0   150 kilometers

16

0   200 miles
0   200 kilometers

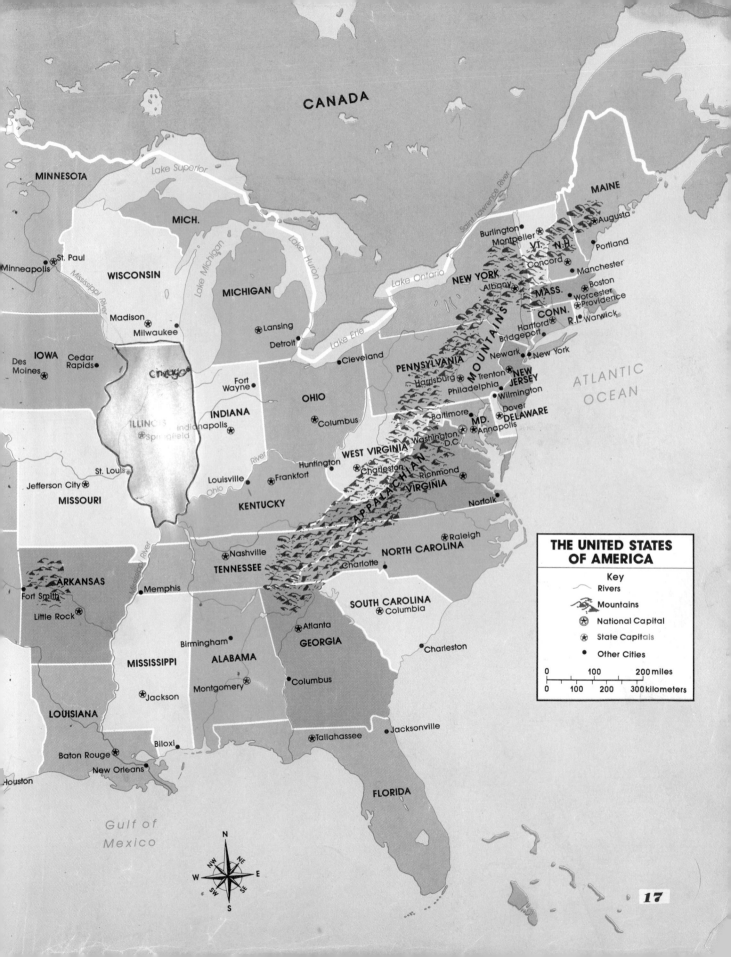

CANADA

MINNESOTA

Lake Superior

MICH.

WISCONSIN

Lake Michigan

Lake Huron

MICHIGAN

• St. Paul
Minneapolis ✪

Mississippi River

Madison ✪
Milwaukee •

✪ Lansing

Detroit •

Lake Erie

Lake Ontario

MAINE

Burlington •
Montpelier ✪
VT.   N.H.
Concord ✪
Augusta ✪
Portland •
Manchester •

Saint Lawrence River

NEW YORK
Albany ✪
MASS.
Boston ✪
Worcester •
CONN.
Providence •
Hartford ✪
R.I. Warwick •
Bridgeport •

IOWA
Des
Moines ✪   Cedar
Rapids •

Chicago

Fort
Wayne •

OHIO

ILLINOIS
Springfield ✪
Indianapolis ✪
INDIANA

Columbus ✪

PENNSYLVANIA
Harrisburg ✪
Philadelphia •
Trenton ✪
NEW
JERSEY
Newark •   New York •
Wilmington •
Dover ✪
MD.   DELAWARE

MOUNTAINS

ATLANTIC
OCEAN

St. Louis •

Jefferson City ✪

MISSOURI

River

Louisville •
Frankfort ✪

KENTUCKY

Ohio   River

Huntington •

WEST VIRGINIA
Charleston ✪

Baltimore •
Washington, ✪
D.C.
Annapolis ✪

APPALACHIAN

VIRGINIA
Richmond ✪

Norfolk •

Nashville ✪

Memphis •

TENNESSEE

Charlotte •

NORTH CAROLINA

Raleigh ✪

ARKANSAS

Fort Smith •

Little Rock ✪

Mississippi River

Birmingham •

MISSISSIPPI   ALABAMA

Jackson ✪   Montgomery ✪

Atlanta ✪

GEORGIA

Columbus •

SOUTH CAROLINA
Columbia ✪

Charleston •

LOUISIANA

Biloxi •

Baton Rouge ✪
New Orleans •

Houston •

Tallahassee ✪

Jacksonville •

FLORIDA

Gulf of
Mexico

N
NW   NE
W   E
SW   SE
S

THE UNITED STATES
OF AMERICA

Key
〜〜〜 Rivers
⛰ Mountains
✪ National Capital
✪ State Capitals
• Other Cities

0   100   200 miles
0   100   200   300 kilometers

ARCTIC OCEAN

Bering Sea

ALASKA (U.S.)

GREENLAND (DEN.)

PACIFIC OCEAN

Hudson Bay

CANADA

UNITED STATES OF AMERICA

ATLANTIC OCEAN

MEXICO

Gulf of Mexico

WEST INDIES

CUBA

DOMINICAN REPUBLIC

HAITI

JAMAICA

PUERTO RICO (U.S.)

Caribbean Sea

BELIZE

GUATEMALA

HONDURAS

EL SALVADOR

NICARAGUA

COSTA RICA

PANAMA

CENTRAL AMERICA

SOUTH AMERICA

N
NE
E
NW
SE
W
SW
S

NORTH AMERICA

KEY

U.S.-United States
Den.-Denmark

0   500
Miles

Continents and Hemispheres

┌─ **VOCABULARY** ────────────┐
│ continent   Equator │
│ hemisphere   │
└────────────────────────────┘

Continents Mexico is the name of the country to the south of the United States. Canada is the country to the north. The United States, Canada, and Mexico are all part of the **continent** of North America. A continent is a very large body of land. Look at the map on page 18. You will see that the West Indies and the seven countries of Central America are also part of North America. There are six other continents on the earth. They are South America, Europe, Africa, Asia, Australia, and Antarctica. Find these continents on the map below.

Our country is located on the continent of North America. North America is the third largest continent.

THE EARTH'S CONTINENTS

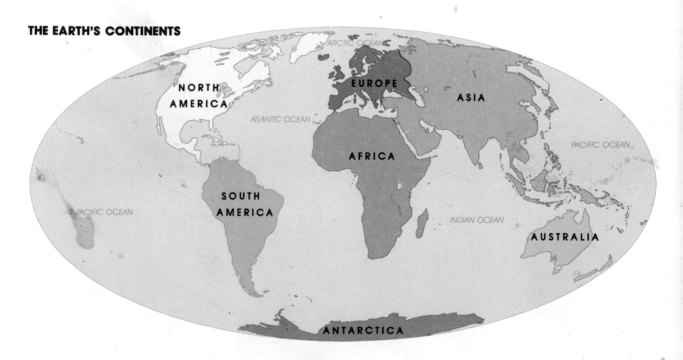

← *The United States is only one country in North America. Name the other countries that are part of the North American continent.*

Along this river on the Equator there is heavy rainfall and much plant growth.

Hemispheres   There are four maps on the next page. Each map shows one half of the earth. A half of the earth is called a **hemisphere** (hem′ ə sfir). The top left map shows the Western Hemisphere. North America is part of the Western Hemisphere. South America is also.

The top right map shows the Eastern Hemisphere. All of Asia and Australia and most of Europe and Africa are in the Eastern Hemisphere.

The **Equator** (i kwā′ tər) is a line that is used on maps. It divides the earth into two other halves. They are the Southern Hemisphere and the Northern Hemisphere. All of Antarctica and Australia are in the Southern Hemisphere. So are parts of Africa and South America and just a small part of Asia. Name the continents in the Northern Hemisphere.

CHECKUP

1. How many continents are there?
2. What continent do we live on?
3. Name the other continents.
4. What is a hemisphere?

20

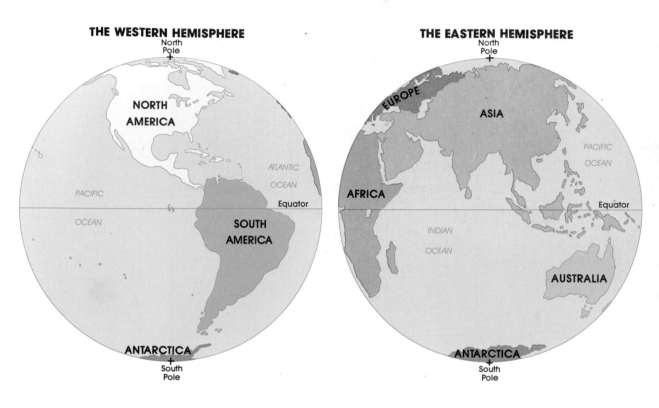

THE WESTERN HEMISPHERE

North
Pole
+

NORTH
AMERICA

ATLANTIC
OCEAN

PACIFIC

Equator

OCEAN

SOUTH
AMERICA

ANTARCTICA
+
South
Pole

THE EASTERN HEMISPHERE

North
Pole
+

EUROPE

ASIA

PACIFIC

OCEAN

AFRICA

Equator

INDIAN

OCEAN

AUSTRALIA

ANTARCTICA
+
South
Pole

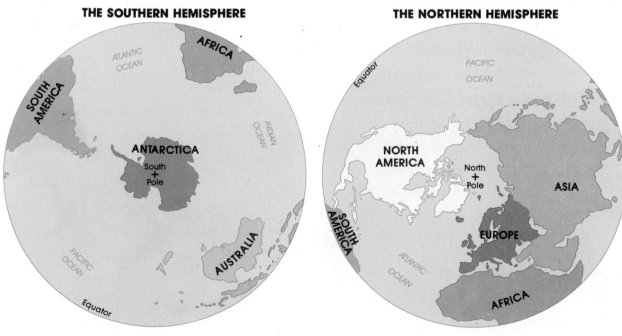

THE SOUTHERN HEMISPHERE

AFRICA

ATLANTIC
OCEAN

SOUTH
AMERICA

INDIAN

OCEAN

ANTARCTICA

South
+
Pole

PACIFIC
OCEAN

AUSTRALIA

Equator

THE NORTHERN HEMISPHERE

Equator

PACIFIC
OCEAN

NORTH
AMERICA

North
+
Pole

ASIA

SOUTH
AMERICA

EUROPE

ATLANTIC
OCEAN

AFRICA

On which continent is the South Pole?

21

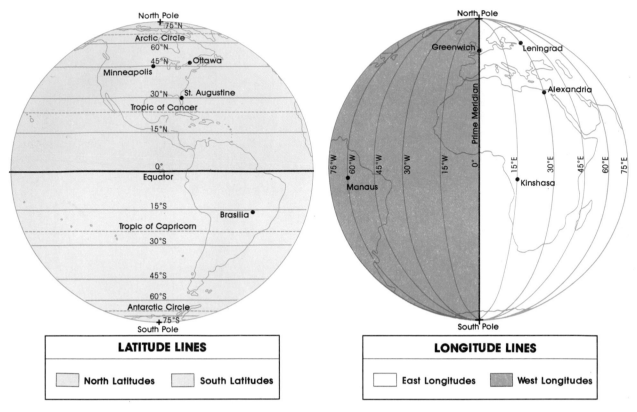

LATITUDE LINES		
North Latitudes	South Latitudes	

LONGITUDE LINES		
East Longitudes	West Longitudes	

The east-west lines on a globe or map are lines of latitude. The lines drawn from the North Pole to the South Pole are lines of longitude.

Latitude and Longitude

┌─**VOCABULARY**──────────────┐

latitude	Tropic of
degree	Capricorn
Arctic Circle	longitude
Antarctic Circle	Prime Meridian
Tropic of	Greenwich
Cancer	

└──────────────────────────────┘

Latitude In order to help us find places on maps, mapmakers use lines of **latitude.** You have already learned about one such line. It is called the Equator. The Equator is halfway between the North Pole and the South Pole. It is a very special line of latitude. It is numbered 0°. All other latitude lines measure distances north or south of the Equator. This distance is measured in **degrees**. The symbol for degrees is °.

Look at the map on the left. You will see that the city of Minneapolis (min ē ap′ ə ləs),

Minnesota, is located at 45 degrees north latitude (45°N). St. Augustine (sānt ô′ gə stēn), Florida, is located near 30 degrees north latitude (30°N).

In addition to the Equator, four other lines of latitude are named. Two of them are the **Arctic Circle** and the **Antarctic Circle.** The Arctic Circle is near the North Pole. The Antarctic Circle is near the South Pole. The coldest parts of the earth are between the Arctic Circle and the North Pole, and between the Antarctic Circle and the South Pole.

The other two named lines of latitude are near the Equator. They are the **Tropic of Cancer** and the **Tropic of Capricorn.** The area between these two lines is called the tropics. Most of the warmest parts of the earth are in the tropics. It is hot all year long in most parts of the tropics.

How hot or cold a place is depends a lot on the latitude. The farther north a place is from the Equator, the colder it is. The closer a place is to the Equator, the hotter it is.

Longitude   Lines of another kind are drawn on maps to help us find places. These are lines of **longitude** (lon′ jə tüd). Look at the right-hand map on page 22. Longitude lines are drawn from the North Pole to the South Pole. A special line of longitude is called the **Prime Meridian** (mə rid′ ē ən). It is numbered 0°. All other longitude lines measure distances east or west of the Prime Meridian. The Prime Meridian passes through a place in England called **Greenwich** (gren′ ich). Half of all longitude lines are west of Greenwich. The other half are east of Greenwich.

Let us find the city of Manaus (mə′ naús), Brazil, on the map. Manaus is in the Western Hemisphere. To make it easier to find, you could tell someone that Manaus is at 60° west longitude on the map.

Now find Leningrad, in the Soviet (sō′ vē et) Union. Leningrad is east of the Prime Meridian. So we say that it is at an east longitude. To be even more exact we can say that it is at 30° east longitude.

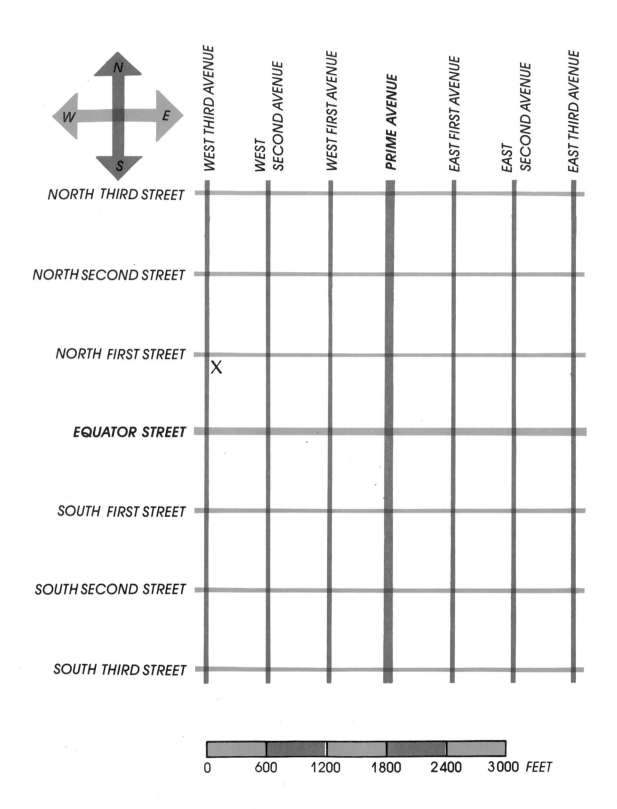

N
W   E
S

WEST THIRD AVENUE
WEST SECOND AVENUE
WEST FIRST AVENUE
PRIME AVENUE
EAST FIRST AVENUE
EAST SECOND AVENUE
EAST THIRD AVENUE

NORTH THIRD STREET

NORTH SECOND STREET

NORTH FIRST STREET

X

EQUATOR STREET

SOUTH FIRST STREET

SOUTH SECOND STREET

SOUTH THIRD STREET

0   600   1200   1800   2400   3000 FEET

Putting it all together Let us see what happens when we put latitude and longitude together. Look at the map on page 24. Think of Equator Street as the Equator. Think of Prime Avenue as the Prime Meridian. Make believe you want to meet some friends at the spot shown on the map by an X. Would it be enough to tell them to meet you on First Street? No, because they would not know whether they were to meet you on North First Street or South First Street. What if you told them to meet you on North First Street? Would that be enough information for your friends? Probably not, because North First Street is a long street. But if you told your friends to meet you at the corner of North First Street and West Third Avenue, they would know exactly where to find you.

← On this map the streets stand for lines of latitude. The avenues stand for lines of longitude.

→ The girls and boys know exactly where to meet. What helps them find the right place?

25

Lines of latitude and longitude are important because they help us find places exactly on a map or globe.

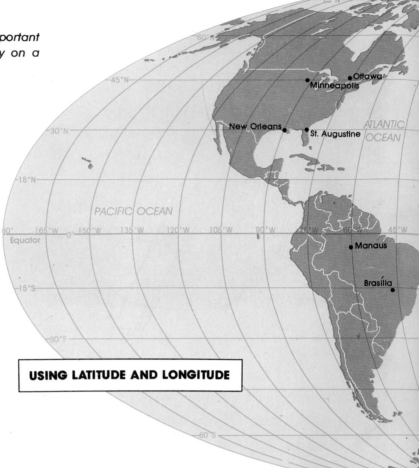

USING LATITUDE AND LONGITUDE

Look at the map of the world on these two pages. It shows a few cities. The map also has lines of latitude and longitude. These lines help us to find places, just as streets and avenues do. Let's practice finding places on the map using latitude and longitude.

If you wanted to tell someone where to find Leningrad, you could just say that it is in the Soviet Union. However, the Soviet Union is the largest country in the world, so you would have to give more information.

You could say that Leningrad is at 60° north latitude and 30° east longitude. If you know the latitude and longitude of a place, you can easily find it on a map. You do this by finding the place where the line

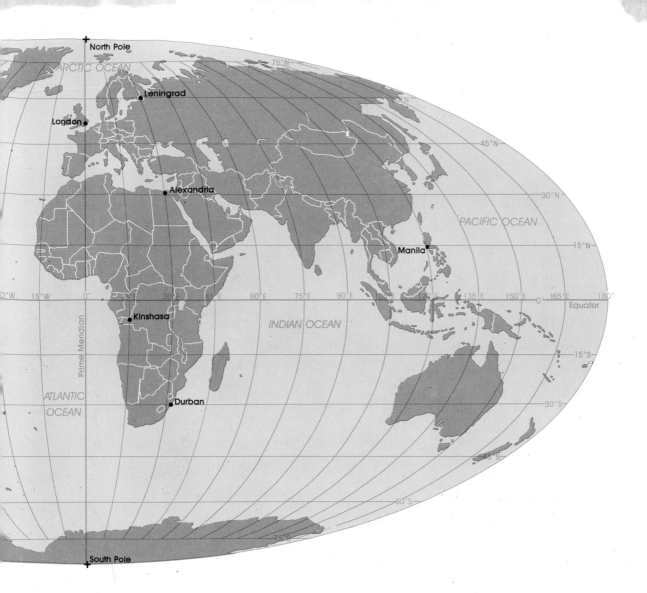

of latitude and the line of longitude cross. To find Leningrad, put one finger on the line marked 60° north latitude. Put a finger of your other hand on the line marked 30° east longitude. Now move your fingers toward each other on these lines. The place where these two lines meet is the location of Leningrad.

Now can you find New Orleans, Louisiana? It is at 30° north latitude and 90° west longitude. Give the longitude and latitude of the other cities on the map.

CHECKUP

1. What do lines of latitude measure?
2. What do lines of longitude measure?

Time Lines

VOCABULARY

time line

When did it happen? Maps and globes are two tools that help you learn more about the world in which you live. A third kind of tool is a **time line.** Maps show us where things are. A time line tells us when certain things happened. Like a map, a time line is a scale drawing.

Look at the time line below. It is 6 inches long. It begins in 1974 and ends in 1986. It shows 12 years in the life of a boy named Ian. Each inch on this time line stands for 2 years in Ian's life. Find the word *Born* on the left of the line. Notice that this word is written above 1974. That means

Ian was born in 1974. Look again at the time line. Find the words *Started School* above the year 1979. Ian started kindergarten in 1979. Do you remember what year you started school? In what year did Ian start third grade?

Many time lines cover more than just 12 years. Look at the time line on page 29. It shows some of the important dates in the history of our country. On this time line each inch stands for 100 years. In what year did the Pilgrims land at Plymouth? What happened in 1492?

CHECKUP

1. What does a time line tell you?
2. What is the scale of the time line shown on page 29?
3. In what year did the Civil War end?

A time line is a scale drawing. What is the scale on this time line?

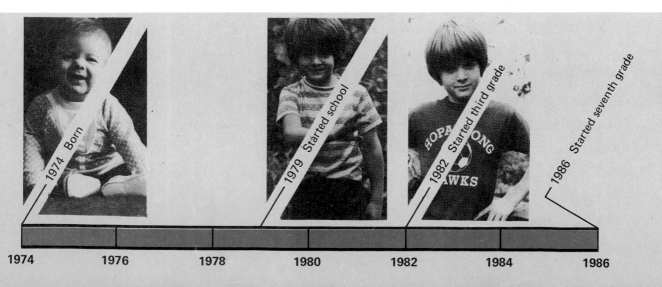

1974 Born

1979 Started school

1982 Started third grade

1986 Started seventh grade

1974 1976 1978 1980 1982 1984 1986

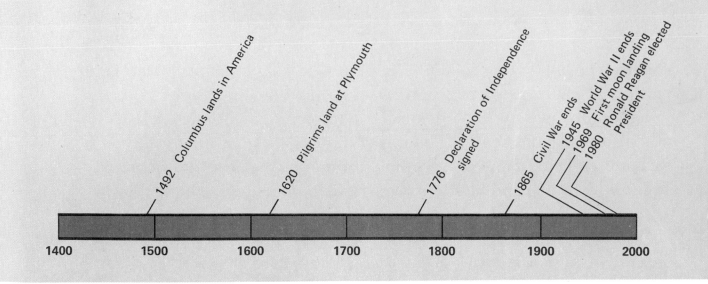

A time line tells when things happened. When did World War II end?

Graphs

VOCABULARY

census
pictograph
pie graph
bar graph
line graph

How much? A fourth kind of tool that can help you learn more about the world in which you live is a graph. A graph can show you *how much, how many,* or *how fast.* It can also show *how much more, how many more,* or *how much faster.*

Knowing how to read a graph is an important social studies skill. It is a skill everyone should have. Sometimes graphs can tell you something more easily than words can.

Ever since 1790, the United States has taken a **census** every ten years. A census is a count of the number of people living in a country. Today, there are more than 229 million people living in the United States. The table below tells you how many people were living in the United States during each of our first five censuses. You can easily see how our population has grown.

UNITED STATES POPULATION: 1790—1830

Year	Number of People
1790	3,929,625
1800	5,308,483
1810	7,239,881
1820	9,638,453
1830	12,866,020

Pictographs One kind of graph is called a **pictograph**. A pictograph uses symbols instead of numerals. Look at the graph below. Notice that each symbol stands for one million people. Four symbols are shown for 1790. That means that there were about 4 million people living in the United States in 1790.

If you are looking for exact numbers, a table would be more helpful than a graph. But the best thing about a graph is the way it shows relationships. That is, it shows how big one thing is compared to another. In a way a graph is like a picture. Just a quick look at the graph on this page shows you which group is the biggest and which is the smallest. You can easily see which groups have about the same number of people. To get that kind of information from the table, you must look more carefully. Turn to page 29 and compare the table to this graph.

A pictograph shows information by using symbols or figures instead of numerals. What does each symbol stand for on this pictograph?

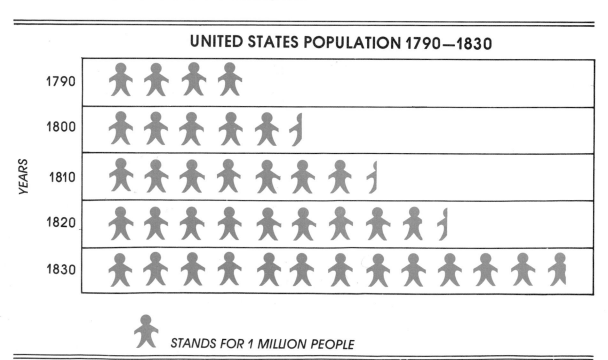

UNITED STATES POPULATION 1790–1830

STANDS FOR 1 MILLION PEOPLE

UNITED STATES POPULATION IN 1790

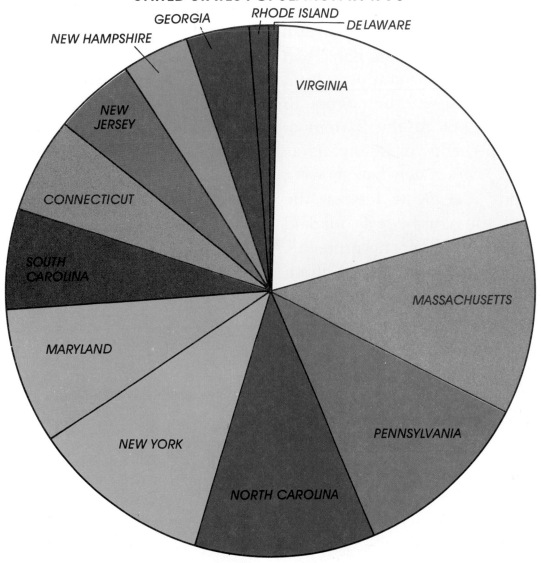

Can you see why this graph is called a pie graph?

Pie graphs   This graph is called a **pie graph.** You can see why. A pie graph tells you how much of one thing there is in a whole. In this graph, the whole pie stands for the whole population of the United States in 1790. This pie is not cut into equal parts. That is because it shows how all of these people were divided among the 13 states that made up our country in 1790. Which state had the most people? Which had the least?

Bar graphs A **bar graph** shows information in bars. You have to read a bar graph up from the bottom and then across to the side. Look at the bottom of the graph shown below. It is marked *Years.* Each bar shows a different year. Now look at the side of the graph. It is marked *Millions of People.* The numerals show how many people there were. Find the bar for 1790. Run your finger up the bar to the top. Now move your finger from the top of the bar to the left. You will see that in 1790 there were about 4 million people living in the United States.

Now look at the bar for 1830. Run your finger up the bar and then across to the side. Your finger should be about halfway between the top line of the graph and the line that stands for 12 million people. What was the population of the United States in 1820? Check your answer with the table on page 29.

This bar graph shows the information in bars. What was the population of the United States in 1800?

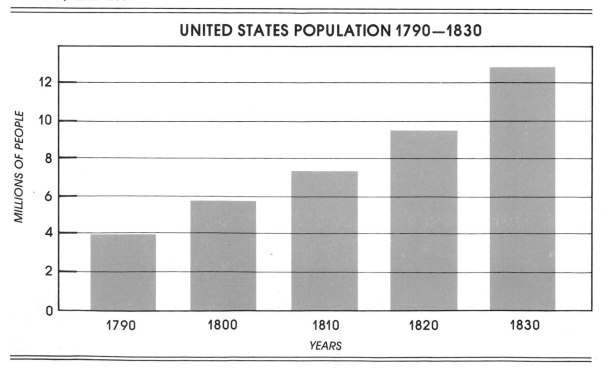

UNITED STATES POPULATION 1790—1830

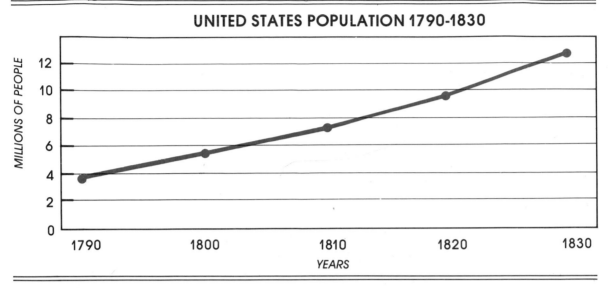

UNITED STATES POPULATION 1790-1830

This line graph gives the same information as the pictograph on page 30 and the bar graph on page 32. What do the dots stand for on the line graph?

Line graphs   Reading a **line graph** is much like reading a bar graph. Look at the line graph above. Notice that it is set up in the same way that the bar graph is set up. That is, the years are shown at the bottom and the number of people is shown at the side. The dots show how many people were counted for each census. Find the dot for 1800. You will see that there were about 5 million people in the United States in 1800. Where is the dot for the year 1810?

Graphs are often used to show a relationship, or connection, between two things. On this line graph the two related things are years and numbers of people.

There is a special graph section on pages 217—225. The graphs show information in different ways. Some of the information is about the United States. Some of it is about other countries. Look at the graphs to see the kinds of information they show.

CHECKUP

1. Which kind of graph uses symbols?
2. When is a table more helpful than a graph?
3. What kind of graph is in the shape of a circle?
4. How do you read a bar graph?

I/CHAPTER REVIEW

KEY FACTS

1. A globe is a model of the earth.
2. Maps show what the earth or parts of the earth look like.
3. The key and its symbols help explain what the map is showing.
4. The scale on a map shows how far one place is from another.
5. Directions and lines of latitude and longitude help locate places on a map.

VOCABULARY QUIZ

Copy the sentences below and fill in the blanks with the right vocabulary term. Write on a sheet of paper.

a. time line   f. physical features
b. latitude   g. border
c. symbols   h. scale
d. coastline   i. Equator
e. compass rose   j. globe

1. The ____ is a model of the earth.
2. A ____ is a scale drawing that tells when things happened.
3. Map ____ stand for real things and places.
4. A small drawing on a map that shows direction is called a ____ .
5. The map ____ tells how far one place is from another.
6. The states of Montana and Vermont ____ on Canada.
7. Rivers, lakes, and mountains are all parts of the earth and are called ____ .
8. The state of Maine has a ____ along the Atlantic Ocean.
9. The ____ is halfway between the North Pole and the South Pole.
10. Lines that run east and west on maps are called lines of ____ .

REVIEW QUESTIONS

1. What do we call a body of land with water all around it?
2. Why is a state capital a special kind of city?
3. Tell what the Great Plains looks like.
4. List the continents of the world.
5. Where are the coldest parts of the earth? Where are the warmest parts?

ACTIVITY

Locate all of the states that have a coastline along the Atlantic Ocean, the Gulf of Mexico, or the Pacific Ocean. Use this information to make a chart like the one shown below. The map on pages 16 – 17 will help you fill in your chart.

Coastlines of States

Atlantic Ocean	Gulf of Mexico	Pacific Ocean

I / SKILLS DEVELOPMENT

USING THE ATLAS AND THE GAZETTEER

THE ATLAS

Your book has a special section called the Atlas. The Atlas is made up of different maps. These maps tell many interesting things about the world in which you live.

SKILLS PRACTICE

The paragraphs below deal with the Atlas. Read each paragraph and answer the numbered questions on a separate sheet of paper.

Turn to the first map in the Atlas on pages 206–207. It is a flat map of the world. It shows the seven continents and the countries on each continent.

1. Name at least four physical features that are shown on the map.

Now look at the two smaller maps below the world map. Those maps are called *insets*. An inset shows a part of the big map. It gives more detail. For example, locate the West Indies on the world map. Notice that the West Indies has lines drawn around it. The words on the map tell you to "see inset below." Look carefully at the inset of the West Indies.

2. What information do you find on the inset that you cannot find on the world map?

Turn now to the second map in the Atlas. It is titled "The United States of America." The map shows lines of latitude and longitude for every five degrees. Name the city found at or near the following lines of latitude and longitude.

3. 35° north latitude and 90° west longitude (35° N/90° W)

4. 40° north latitude and 105° west longitude (40° N/105° W)

THE GAZETTEER

Another special section in your book is called the Gazetteer. This is a dictionary of geographical names and is arranged alphabetically. The Gazetteer gives information about cities, rivers, mountains, and other physical features. It also shows latitude and longitude for cities.

SKILLS PRACTICE

Turn to the Gazetteer, starting on page 226, and answer the questions.

1. What is the latitude and longitude of Portland, Oregon?

2. On what river is London found?

3. Where does the Columbia River start?

4. What is special about the city of St. Augustine?

2 Studying Your Community

Using Maps

> **VOCABULARY**
> soldier
> dog guide

A class learns about its community In the last chapter you learned that we all live in communities. Each of you may think that your community is the most important. The truth is that all communities are important. They all have special people and places.

This book will be read in schools all across the United States. We cannot study all of our communities. There are too many. So we will learn how one group of students studied their community. This will show us some ways to study our own community.

We are going to look at a class of girls and boys who go to Alfred Vail School. It is in Morris Township, New Jersey. Find New Jersey on the map on pages 16–17. What states are next to New Jersey?

Some of the students at Alfred Vail School live in Morris Township. Other students live in the community of Morristown. The two communities are side by side. The children from both communities go to the same schools together.

Getting started This year the students said they wanted to learn more about their communities. Their teacher, Mrs. Reilly, asked them what they already knew about Morristown and Morris Township. The children knew a lot. They knew that George Washington and some of his **soldiers** had stayed in Morristown many years ago. They knew that some people from their community work in

This aerial photograph shows the center of Morristown, New Jersey.

stores in Morristown and Morris Township while others travel by car or train to work in New York City. They knew about the school in Morristown that trains **dog guides** for blind people.

"We have talked about some of the things we know about our communities," said Mrs. Reilly. "Now please think of something in your community that you would like to study. It might be something that is new to you. Or it might be something that you want to learn more about."

Mrs. Reilly then asked the students to tell her what they wanted to study. This helped her group the class so that students with the same interests could work together. Next Mrs. Reilly met with the girls and boys in each group. They talked about what they would do and how they could learn more about their subject.

We will look now at each group to see how they studied and what they learned about their community.

(Left) Everyone is busy in Mrs. Reilly's classroom. (Right) Chris fills in a map of the United States.

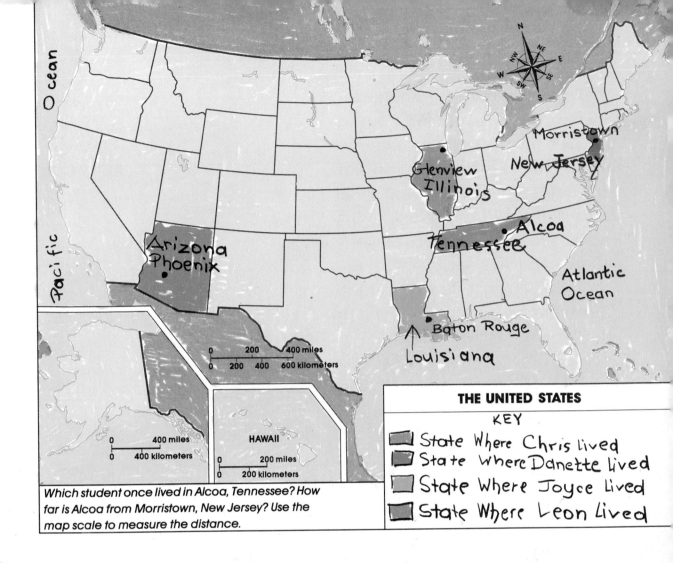

Ocean

Pacific

Arizona
Phoenix

Glenview
Illinois

Morristown
New Jersey

Alcoa
Tennessee

Atlantic
Ocean

Baton Rouge
Louisiana

0   200   400 miles
0   200   400   600 kilometers

0   400 miles
0   400 kilometers

HAWAII

0   200 miles
0   200 kilometers

Which student once lived in Alcoa, Tennessee? How far is Alcoa from Morristown, New Jersey? Use the map scale to measure the distance.

THE UNITED STATES

KEY

State Where Chris lived

State Where Danette lived

State Where Joyce lived

State Where Leon Lived

Making maps Chris, Danette, Leon, and Joyce had moved to New Jersey during the summer. They wanted to make maps. These maps would help them find places. They decided to make four maps. Mrs. Reilly gave them some maps to use. These maps showed the outlines of certain places. They also showed a compass rose and a scale of miles. The girls and boys had to fill in the maps and make map keys.

Chris filled in a map of the United States. He named New Jersey. He also named the states and the communities where he, Danette, Joyce, and Leon used to live. Look at Chris's map on this page. Where did he live before moving to New Jersey?

Danette wanted to show New Jersey. She located Morristown on her map. She also showed other cities in the state and how far they are from Morristown. She traced over the two rivers named on the map. Danette's map is shown on this page.

Joyce's map showed Morris Township and Morristown and the many other communities nearby. She colored Morristown and Morris Township different colors on the map. She showed what the colors stood for in the

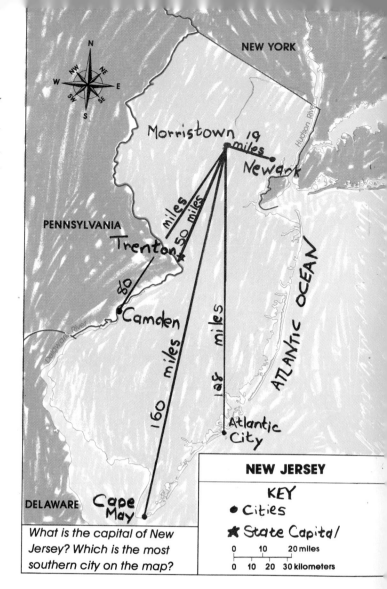

Morristown 19 miles
Newark
PENNSYLVANIA
Trenton
miles
50 miles
80
Camden
160 miles
35 miles
ATLANTIC OCEAN
Atlantic City
DELAWARE
Cape May
Hudson River
Delaware River
NEW YORK

NEW JERSEY
KEY
• Cities
★ State Capital
0   10   20 miles
0   10   20   30 kilometers

What is the capital of New Jersey? Which is the most southern city on the map?

Danette points to Morristown in New Jersey.

map key. Look at Joyce's map at the top of the opposite page. Find Morristown and Morris Township.

Leon mapped Morristown and Morris Township. He named some of the main streets and highways. He colored the lakes blue. He showed where some important places are located. He

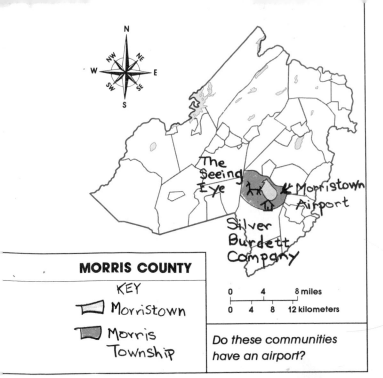

MORRIS COUNTY

KEY

⬜ Morristown

🟪 Morris Township

0   4   8 miles
0   4   8   12 kilometers

Do these communities have an airport?

also placed his home and school on the map. Leon's map is at the bottom of this page. Look at the key that Leon made. On which street does Leon live?

CHECKUP

1. Which states border on New Jersey?
2. What information did Chris's map show?
3. How was Danette's map different from Joyce's map?
4. Does Morristown have a hospital?

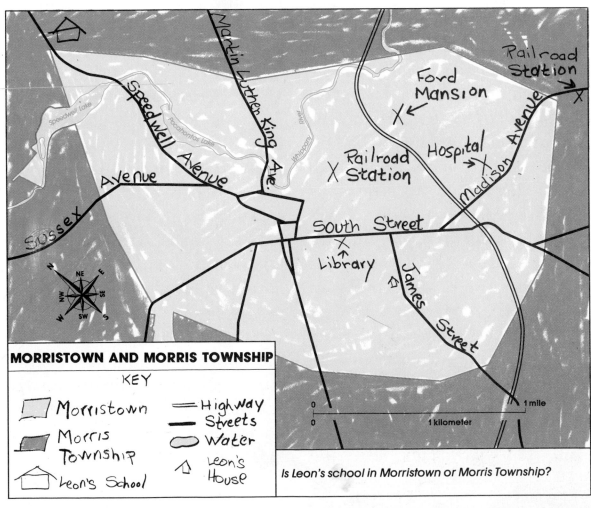

MORRISTOWN AND MORRIS TOWNSHIP

KEY

⬜ Morristown

🟪 Morris Township

🏠 Leon's School

═ Highway

— Streets

⬭ Water

🏠 Leon's House

Is Leon's school in Morristown or Morris Township?

41

Learning About the Past

Courtesy of the Harvard University Portrait Collection

George Washington was the first President of the United States.

A national park   Gail, Danny, Kristin, and Dennis wanted to learn more about a special place in their community. It is the Morristown National Historical Park. A **national park** belongs to all the people of a country. In this national park is a house named the Ford Mansion. George Washington stayed here more than two hundred years ago. Fort Nonsense is also part of the national park. Washington had his soldiers build this fort on a high hill in Morristown. A third part of the park is Jockey Hollow. This is where many of Washington's soldiers camped. It is located a few miles from the center of Morristown.

"We know what we want to study," said Danny. "But how can we find out about things that happened so long ago?"

"We can use books," answered Gail. "And we can visit the national park," said Dennis. Kristin was happy. "I have a new camera and will take some pictures of the park."

Using library books   First the students decided to use books to learn more about the national park. So they went to the school library. There they talked with the librarian, Mrs. Lewis. She showed them how to look for books in the card catalog. This is an alphabetical list of the books in the library. Then Mrs. Lewis showed the students how to find the books on the shelves. They found six books about George Washington. Only two of the books had information about Morristown.

Mrs. Lewis also told the boys and girls to look in the encyclopedias. "These books have a lot of information about many different things. You will find them on special shelves in the library."

The students found several different sets of encyclopedias. They looked up the name *George Washington* in the encyclopedia marked *W*. The girls and boys found information they could use. They also looked up information under the headings *Revolutionary War, New Jersey,* and *Morristown.*

Visiting the park   After they had gathered all the information they could find in books, the students visited the national park. They were given some booklets. These told them about the park and the things that happened there. They walked through the Ford Mansion and the **museum** behind the house. A museum is a building where people may see many interesting things on display. The students also walked around Jockey Hollow and Fort Nonsense. At each place Kristin took pictures with her camera. The other students made notes about the different things they saw.

Together the girls and boys wrote a report about the national park. They explained some of the things they had learned. They used pictures they had taken at the park to make their report more interesting. This is their report.

The librarian helps the students find information in the encyclopedia. The boys and girls will use the information to write a report.

THE MORRISTOWN NATIONAL HISTORICAL PARK

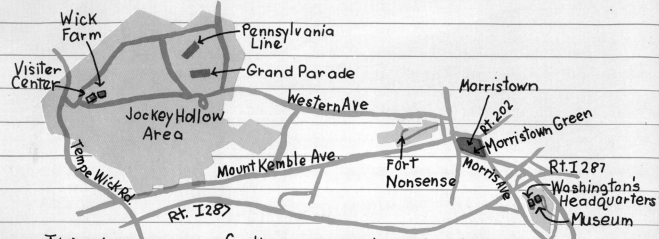

This is a map of the national park. Many people visit this park each year. They come from all over the country.

THE FORD MANSION

The Ford Mansion was built in 1772. Colonel Jacob Ford had the house built. He owned iron mines near Morristown. He also had a powder mill. The mill made gunpowder. This gunpowder was important to the Americans during the Revolutionary War.

This war took place between 1775 and 1781. The American people wanted to be free from English rule. So they decided to fight for their freedom. George Washington was made the leader of the American army. Some battles were fought near Morristown.

General Washington stayed at the Ford Mansion from December 1779 to June 1780. It served as his headquarters. Here he planned the last years of the war.

The Ford Mansion has been made to look like it did when General Washington stayed there. One of the most interesting places in the house was the kitchen. As many as 18 people could stay close to its warm fires.

THE HISTORICAL MUSEUM
The museum is behind the Ford Mansion. It has many books and papers. It also has several models. These models show what life was like long ago. There is a famous picture of George Washington. There are many old guns in cabinets for people to see.

FORT NONSENSE

The lay of the land

Fort Nonsense was built on the top of a high hill in Morristown. From this hill you could see for miles. General Washington had his soldiers build the fort in 1777. Today there is nothing left of the fort.

JOCKEY HOLLOW

Washington's army spent the winter of 1779-1780 at Jockey Hollow. About 13,000 soldiers stayed here. They built more than 1,100 cabins. They used wood from oak, walnut, and chestnut trees. Every cabin was about 14 feet wide and 15 feet long. The cabins all had bunk beds and fireplaces. Twelve soldiers lived in each cabin.

The winter of 1779-1780 was very cold. There was a lot of snow. The soldiers did not have enough warm clothing. They were often hungry. General Washington asked the people of New

Jersey for help. The people of our state gave food that helped save the army.

Today there are many things to see at Jockey Hollow. The first place we visited was the Tempe Wick House. It was built in 1750. It still looks like it did long ago. We heard a story here. The Wicks had a daughter named Tempe. She hid her horse in her bedroom once to keep it from being stolen by soldiers

Near the Wick House are some cabins. They are built like the ones the soldiers built. We went into the cabin that served as a hospital. We learned about the kind of care that was given to General Washington's soldiers.

Soldiers' cabins at Jockey Hollow

CHECKUP

1. In what two ways did the students learn about famous places in their community?
2. Why is the Ford Mansion important?
3. What did the cabins at Jockey Hollow look like?
4. Who gave food to the American soldiers during the winter of 1779—1780?

Working in a Community

```
┌─VOCABULARY─────────────────────┐
│  area                 product  │
│  chamber of                    │
│     commerce                   │
└────────────────────────────────┘
```

Writing for information Bill, Joe, and Shelly wanted to learn about places to work in the Morristown **area.** Area is the land for several miles around a community. Bill said he would like to find out what some of the companies make. Joe and Shelly decided they would like to learn a lot about one company.

Bill said to Mrs. Reilly, "There are so many companies to learn about. Where do I start?"

Mrs. Reilly answered, "You might write the **chamber of commerce**. This is a group of business people. They should have some information about the companies and their **products.** A product is something that a company makes.

"You will find the address for the chamber of commerce in the telephone book. Send your letter to Mr. Como. He will be glad to help you."

Bill shows his best handwriting in this letter.

139 Elm Street
Morristown, New Jersey 07960
September 25, 1984

Mr. Elliott Como
Morris County Chamber of Commerce
330 South Street
Morristown, New Jersey 07960

Dear Mr. Como:

My class at Alfred Vail School is studying the community we live in. I want to learn about businesses in the Morristown area.

Please send me any information you have. I am really interested in finding out about the many different things these companies do.

Thank you for your help.

Sincerely,
Bill Snyder

Making a chart   Three days later, Bill received a package in the mail. The package was from Mr. Como. It was full of material about companies in and near Morristown.

Bill found that there are some very big companies in and near Morristown. There are also some small companies. There were so many places of business that he could not learn about each of them. So he decided to make a chart to show some of the largest companies in the area. Bill showed what the companies made or did. You can see Bill's chart below.

BUSINESSES IN THE MORRISTOWN AREA

Company	Workers	Products
Jersey Central Power and Light	3,021	Electricity
Allied Corporation	2,300	Chemicals and plastics
Warner Lambert	2,200	Health-care products
Crum and Forster	1,100	Insurance
Monroe Calculator	850	Calculators
Mennen Company	725	Health and beauty aids
Silver Burdett	278	School textbooks
Diamond Shamrock	260	Chemicals

Visiting a company   Joe and Shelly told Mrs. Reilly that they wanted to learn a lot about one company. Mrs. Reilly asked if there was a company that they wanted to study. Shelly answered, "Yes. We saw that some of our books are made by a company located in Morris Township. I think its name is Silver Burdett Company. It would be fun to see how our books are made."

Mrs. Reilly called Silver Burdett Company. She talked with Miss Teffeau (tə fō′). She is an editor. She helps the people who write the books. Miss Teffeau said that she would be happy to have Shelly and Joe visit.

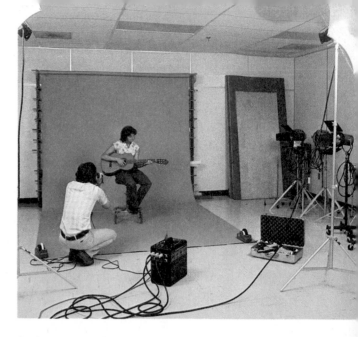

A photographer uses a camera and other kinds of equipment to take pictures.

Miss Teffeau was waiting for them when they arrived. "I want to tell you about our company," she said. "We make books. These books are used in schools all across our country. They are also used in other countries. Mrs. Reilly told you that we do not print books here. Our books are printed by companies in other states. We do everything but print the books in this building.

"I am an editor," Miss Teffeau explained. "I work with the authors. Authors are the people who write the books. I also work with mapmakers and photographers, people who take pictures."

Editors check a map of the United States.

Miss Teffeau told Joe and Shelly about the way their textbooks were made. She said, "Each book has at least one author. He or she writes one chapter at a time and sends it to an editor. The editor then sends each chapter to readers and the authors of other books. These people are asked for ways to improve the book. The readers are often teachers in different states. Sometimes we even have students read the chapters for us. The author will then rewrite parts of the book to make it better.

"The author and the editor work together to make the books attractive," Miss Teffeau said. "The author usually tells the editor what pictures, maps, or drawings to put in the book. The editor then works with people in the art department.

"These people help make our books ones that students want to open and read. They find the pictures and maps that the authors want for the books. They work with artists, mapmakers, and photographers.

"Well, that is the tour of our building," said Miss Teffeau. "I hope you enjoyed it."

The next day, Joe and Shelly wrote about their visit to Silver Burdett. In their report, they told about the many things they had learned from a book company.

This is a book designer at Silver Burdett Company. He plans where the words and pictures go on the pages of a book.

CHECKUP

1. How did Bill gather his information about businesses in the Morristown area? How did he show this information?
2. Name some of the different kinds of workers at Silver Burdett Company.

The Seeing Eye—A Very Special Place

Dog guides Betty, David, Susan, and Tommy wanted to learn more about **The Seeing Eye.** This is a school that trains dog guides for blind people. It is located near Morristown.

Bonnie is David's big sister. She helps raise and train the dogs. This is one of her 4-H club projects. The 4-H clubs find ways to help their communities. David told Betty, Susan, and Tommy about his sister. "Bonnie is in high school. Every year she gets a new puppy. She feeds the puppy and takes care of it. She even helps train it. The puppies stay with us for a year. After a year, The Seeing Eye takes back the dog and gives Bonnie another puppy."

"I have seen some people in town walking with dogs," said Betty. "Mom told me that the dogs were guides for blind people. Let us see if Bonnie can come to our class and tell us about The Seeing Eye."

Bonnie told David, "Sure, I would love to talk to your class. Why don't I call Mr. Whitstock at The Seeing Eye. Then he can send you and your friends some information. Mr. Whitstock might even be able to bring one of the trained dogs to the class."

Mr. Whitstock uses a special machine to write braille (brāl). Braille is a code of small raised dots on paper. Mr. Whitstock and other blind persons read braille by running their fingers along on the raised dots.

Betty, David, Susan, and Tommy received the material from The Seeing Eye in the mail. Mr. Whitstock also called and told David that he would really like to visit their class. He asked David if he and his friends would read the material and tell the other students about The Seeing Eye. Mr. Whitstock said that he and Bonnie would answer any questions that the class might want to ask.

Raising the puppies Just before Mr. Whitstock and Bonnie came to their class, the students reported on The Seeing Eye.

David told the class about raising puppies for The Seeing Eye.

"Most of the puppies that become dog guides are born at The Seeing Eye breeding station. By the time they are three months old, they are placed in homes. The puppies are given to boys and girls who are members of 4-H clubs. The boys and girls raise the puppies for about a year. They teach the puppies to behave. They also teach them such things as how to climb stairs and get along with people.

"Last year, my sister and her puppy did a lot of different things. They went on a bus ride

Most of the puppies that become dog guides are born at The Seeing Eye.

A 4-H club member gets a puppy to raise for The Seeing Eye. Boys and girls who join 4-H clubs learn useful skills. They also learn to serve their communities.

with other 4-H members and their puppies. They went to the airport and took their puppies into an airplane.

"Another time they walked around town. They took their puppies into stores and other buildings. They even took the puppies for a ride in an elevator. My sister said that she and her puppy learned a lot. One thing she learned was not to take dogs on escalators in stores. Their paws might get caught in the moving stairs."

The first dog-guide school
Betty told the class some facts about The Seeing Eye. She said, "The Seeing Eye began in 1929. It is the oldest dog-guide school in North America. It has placed over 8,000 dogs with more than 5,000 people.

"Any blind person may ask for a dog. They have to pay about $150. This pays for the dog, the equipment, and the training at the school in Morristown. It also pays for the blind person's travel to and from Morristown."

Training the dogs Tommy reported on the training of the dogs. He told the class, "The blind people do not train their own dogs. The dogs are trained by instructors who have spent 2 years learning how to train dogs.

An instructor teaches a dog how to behave in a department store. This is part of its training as a dog guide.

"The dogs are about 14 months old when they are trained. It takes about 3 months to train a dog guide.

"The dog is first taught to obey. It must learn commands such as "forward," "sit," "right," and "left." The dog must also learn to disobey a command if it would put the blind person in danger. A dog guide will not cross a busy street unless cars and trucks have stopped."

A dog guide wears a special harness. It has a handle for the blind person to use while walking.

A blind person learns how to work with her dog guide. An instructor follows behind them. He wants to be sure the blind person gives the right commands and follows her dog.

The Seeing Eye school

Susan told the class about The Seeing Eye school. "The school shows the blind people how to work with their dogs. It usually takes a month for the people to learn everything they need to know.

"Each blind person has to learn how to take care of the dog. The owner has to learn how to follow the dog and how to give commands. The dog and the blind person need to work together. More than 200 blind people are trained every year."

This woman is a dark-room technician at a hospital. Her dog guide goes everywhere with her.

The Seeing Eye has more than 250 puppies living with 4-H club members.

Help wanted When Susan finished her report, she introduced Bonnie. Bonnie told the class, "There are more than 250 puppies living with 4-H club members. We really want more members to help raise the puppies. We would like to raise 300 puppies each year.

"Right now, 4-H club members all over New Jersey are raising puppies. There are also club members in Pennsylvania who have some puppies. Members from 9 to 19 years old raise the puppies. There are some adults who raise puppies, too.

"Mr. Whitstock is outside with a dog guide named Juno. Before they come in, I have a surprise for you. I want you to meet Freddy. He is the next puppy that I am going to raise. In a little over a year he will be trained just like Juno."

At this time, Mr. Whitstock came into the room led by Juno. Mr. Whitstock answered all of the students' questions. He explained that the greatest problem the dog owners have is with people who want to pet or talk to the dog. "This takes the dog's mind off its job," he said.

Mr. Whitstock asked if any members of the class would like to raise a puppy. He told the students to have their parents call him. "We really do need more people who will make a good home for these puppies."

CHECKUP

1. In what ways do 4-H club members help train the puppies?
2. How may a blind person get a dog guide?
3. What are some things that a dog guide must learn?
4. What is one of the greatest problems dog-guide owners have?

Having Fun in a Community

Parks and playgrounds
Allen, Cheryl, Diane, and Barbara decided to find out about places to have fun in the Morristown area.

"Barbara and I want to learn about community parks and playgrounds," said Diane. "Let's ask Mrs. Reilly where to look for information."

Mrs. Reilly told the girls about her neighbor, Mrs. Garcia. "Mrs. Garcia helps plan the new parks. Maybe you can visit her. I'll telephone her tonight."

The girls wanted to use a tape recorder. That way they could record their talk with Mrs. Garcia. The first thing they did was learn how to run the tape machine. Next they made a list of questions to ask Mrs. Garcia in the **interview.** They wanted to ask good questions so that Mrs. Garcia would give interesting answers.

A few days later Diane and Barbara visited Mrs. Garcia. After their talk, the girls wrote answers to some of the questions. Here is part of the interview.

Barbara and Diane use a tape recorder when they interview Mrs. Garcia.

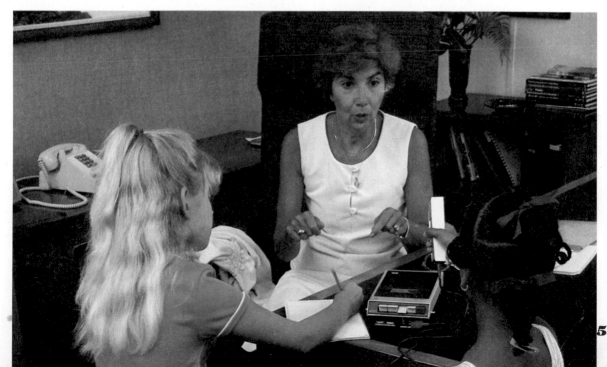

An Interview with Mrs. Garcia

Barbara: We know there are many parks and playgrounds in our town already. Are there any plans for new ones?

Mrs. Garcia: The people in our community and the nearby areas want to spend more time outside. So there is a special group of people who plan new parks. We met just last month to plan a new bicycle path. This path will be four miles long. It will run beside a stream.

Are there any bicycle paths in your community?

Diane: What are some things that people do when they go to the parks?

Mrs. Garcia: At Lewis Morris Park, people can go swimming. They can have picnics and play softball. There are hiking trails and fireplaces for cookouts. In another park, people can go horseback riding.

When it snows, some people like to go cross-country skiing in the parks. Other people like to ice-skate. Everyone seems to enjoy our parks.

Diane: Will there still be parks when we grow up?

Mrs. Garcia: Most of the parks are owned by the community or the state. This means that they belong to all of us. We are always trying to buy more land for parks. Last year someone even gave us land for a park. We may never have as many as we would like to have. But there will be parks when you grow up.

Things to do Allen and Cheryl wanted to know where they could go with their friends on weekends. They asked their parents about different things to do and places to visit around Morristown. They made a list of the places their parents named. It was a long list!

Then Allen and Cheryl asked their friends for pictures of some of the places. Allen explained to Mrs. Reilly, "We want to make a bulletin-board display with all the pictures we have. That way everybody can see where they may go to have fun."

Here are some of the pictures.

It is fun to ride a horse or speed down a mountain slide.

On your own   In this chapter you have read how one class studied about its community. These girls and boys learned many interesting things.

Now it is your turn to learn some things about your own community. As you study your community, you should try to answer some of the questions below. These are not all the questions that can be asked about a city or town. When you think of other questions, write them in a list.

A parade is one way people celebrate their community's history.

People in many communities travel by bus. Buses go from one community to another.

Important Facts

What is the name of my community?

How did my community get its name?

What are the names of nearby communities?

What is the name of my state?

Where is my state located in the United States?

Making a Living

How many people live in my community?

What kinds of jobs do people have?

How do people travel to work?

What are some of the stores and businesses in my community?

The Past

Who were the first people living in my community?

What did my community look like long ago?

Who are some famous people from my community?

What important things have happened in my community?

Skiing is a popular sport in some communities. Is there an area for skiing near your home?

Communities need many different workers. These carpenters are building a motel.

Interesting Places

What are some places that people visit when they are in my community?

Why do people visit these places?

CHECKUP

1. In what ways did Allen, Cheryl, Diane, and Barbara gather information about their community?
2. How did Barbara and Diane get ready for their interview with Mrs. Garcia?

2/CHAPTER REVIEW

KEY FACTS

1. We all live in communities.
2. We can learn about communities by using maps.
3. Many communities have famous places that show much about their past.
4. There are often many different places of business in our communities.
5. All communities have places where people go to learn and to have fun.

VOCABULARY QUIZ

Write the numbers 1 to 10 on a sheet of paper. Match the words in the first part with their meanings in the second part.

a. chamber of commerce
b. national park
c. soldier
d. interview
e. product
f. The Seeing Eye
g. mansion
h. dog guide
i. area
j. museum

1. A very large house
2. A building where people can see many interesting things on display
3. A dog that is specially trained to guide a blind person
4. Something that people make
5. A person who serves in an army
6. A meeting of people face to face to talk over something special
7. Oldest dog-guide school for the blind in North America
8. A group made up of business people who help the community
9. The land for several miles around a community
10. A park that belongs to all the people of a country

REVIEW QUESTIONS

1. What did the students learn about Morristown from Leon's map?
2. How did the students use the library to locate information?
3. Why did Bill write a letter to the chamber of commerce?
4. What are some things that a blind person must learn about a dog guide?

ACTIVITIES

1. List the places in your community that you think a visitor would like to see.
2. If your community has a chamber of commerce, write a class letter to it asking for information.
3. Draw a map of your community. On this map show where some parks and playgrounds are found.
4. Plan a museum for your town or city. List the things that you would put in the museum to help visitors learn about your community.

FINDING THE MAIN IDEA IN A PARAGRAPH

WHAT IS A PARAGRAPH?

Writing is a skill you will use all your life. It is one way to share your ideas with other people. When you write, it is important to put your ideas in order. A paragraph will help you express your ideas clearly.

A paragraph is a group of sentences. The sentences tell about a certain thing. The first sentence is indented, or moved in.

A paragraph begins with a topic sentence. A topic sentence states the main idea. It tells what the paragraph is about. Other sentences explain the main idea. These sentences are called supporting sentences.

YOSEMITE NATIONAL PARK

The paragraph below gives information about a special place in California. Read the paragraph carefully and find the topic sentence and the supporting sentences.

Yosemite (yō sem′ ət ē) National Park has always been a place that people like to visit. Some people come to Yosemite to see the many kinds of wild animals. Others come just to look at its many places of beauty. They stay on the roads around and in the park. Other people hike on the paths and trails. Some camp in tents, in trailers, or under the open sky. People who like the out-of-doors find many things to enjoy in Yosemite.

Now that you have read the paragraph let us look at it closely. What is the main idea of the paragraph? The first sentence tells the main idea. That is, Yosemite is a place people like to visit. The other sentences tell about the reasons why people like to visit Yosemite. The supporting sentences explain the topic sentence.

SKILLS PRACTICE

Now it is your turn to write a paragraph. Read each sentence below. Decide which sentence is the main idea. Write the topic sentence on a sheet of paper. Remember to indent this first sentence. Then write the supporting sentences in the best order for a good paragraph.

They also tell about the wild animals, especially the black bears.

They tell visitors about the plants and the different kinds of rocks.

The rangers of Yosemite National Park have a very important job.

The rangers warn people not to feed the black bears or get too close to them.

I / UNIT REVIEW

1. Models help us learn about the earth. The globe is a model of the earth. — *What are some things that we can learn about the earth from a globe?*

2. Maps are flat drawings of the earth or part of the earth. They help us see what the earth looks like. — *How do each of the following parts of a map help us use maps? (a) key; (b) symbols; (c) compass rose; (d) scale.*

3. The earth is made up of different physical features. Among them are mountains, lakes, and oceans. — *How many different physical features can you find on the map on pages 208–209? Make a list.*

4. Graphs are special drawings that use pictures, circles, bars, and lines to show information. — *Make a pictograph showing how many girls and boys in your class have birthdays in each of the twelve months. Use the pictograph on page 30 to help you make your graph.*

5. A time line tells us when things happened. — *Draw a time line of your day showing what you do and when you do it.*

6. A community is a place where people live, work, and play. — *If you were to make a map of your community, what are some of the things you would show with symbols?*

7. All communities are important. — *Why is your community important? How can you learn more about your community?*

Living in Different Communities

3 Living in Cities

Cities Have a Past

┌─ VOCABULARY ─────────────────┐

valley	port
causeway	climate
natural	weather
resources	temperature
transportation	government city
trade	

└──────────────────────────────┘

How cities began   In Chapter 1 you learned that a city is a large community. Today many people live, work, and play in cities all over the world.

People have not always lived in cities. Long ago people moved from place to place in search of food. They hunted animals and gathered plants to eat.

In time, some people learned to grow plants. Other people learned to raise animals for food. These people became farmers. They began to stay in one place to take care of their plants and animals.

Once they started farming, people found they could often produce more food than they could eat. When this happened, some people were able to stop farming. They started doing other kinds of work, such as making pottery bowls and dishes, or weaving cloth. Little by little, people began to live together in communities. In time, some of these communities grew into small cities.

Tenochtitlán   One community that grew in size was named Tenochtitlán (tā näch tē tlän'). It was built hundreds of years ago by the Aztec (az' tek) Indians. The Aztecs lived in what is now the country of Mexico.

Tenochtitlán was built on an island in the middle of a lake. This lake was in a **valley.** A valley is a lowland between hills or mountains. The Valley of Mexico

The city of San Francisco, California, is at 37 degrees north latitude and 122 degrees west longitude. It began as a Spanish settlement in 1776.

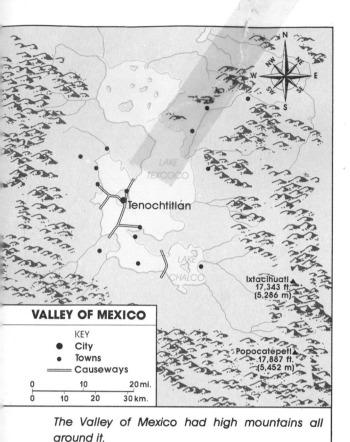

The Valley of Mexico had high mountains all around it.

had high mountains all around it. Many Indians had settled in the area because of the lake water and the rich farmland.

The map on this page shows the Valley of Mexico and the island on which Tenochtitlán was built. The Aztecs connected their island to the land around it by making **causeways.** The causeways were like bridges, but they were made of land.

Over many years Tenochtitlán grew larger as more people came to live and work there. By the time the first people from Europe came to Mexico, there was a big city at Tenochtitlán. It had

This picture shows a model of the Aztec capital Tenochtitlán.

beautiful buildings, wide streets, and room for many people. Look at the photograph on page 70.

All of the communities we live in today were built long after Tenochtitlán began. Let us look at some of the reasons why different cities began and grew.

Important natural resources Some cities began because they were located near important **natural resources.** A natural resource is something useful to people and supplied by nature. You have already learned why the people of Tenochtitlán first settled in that area. They came there because of the lake water and the rich farmland. These are valuable natural resources. Farmers need good land and water in order to grow enough food.

Water is useful for another reason. It gives people a way to travel and to move products from place to place. This is called **transportation.** Many cities have grown up along lakes and rivers because of easy transportation. One such city is Cincinnati, Ohio. Find Cincinnati in the Gazetteer on page 226. The latitude and longitude are given for the city. Use that information to find the city on the map on pages 208–209.

Today Mexico City stands where Tenochtitlán used to be.

Cincinnati About two hundred years ago, Cincinnati began as a small community on the bank of the Ohio River. Here farmers brought their crops to be loaded on boats and shipped to nearby communities along the river. Business people also sent their many products to be sold in communities along the Ohio. In the same way, other river communities shipped their farm and business products by boat to Cincinnati. This buying and selling of products, called **trade**, helped Cincinnati grow. The city became a very busy **port** where boats loaded and unloaded their products.

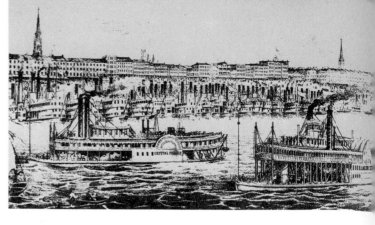

Steamboats carried people and products to Cincinnati.

Cincinnati, Ohio, is located along the Ohio River. It is located at 39 degrees north latitude and 85 degrees west longitude.

Denver There are other natural resources besides land and water that have helped cities grow. Denver, Colorado, began as a small settlement on the South Platte River. It quickly grew into a busy mining town after gold was discovered in the nearby mountains. The gold brought many miners and their families to Colorado. Some people did not find gold. Instead they started farms on the Great Plains. Other people opened stores and sold food and other products to the miners. Soon the main streets of Denver were lined with stores.

Within a few years, silver, lead, and copper had been discovered, too. These natural resources

(Top) Denver is at the place where the Great Plains meet the Rocky Mountains. (Bottom) In 1860 Denver was a busy mining town with a bank and stores of many kinds.

drew still more people to Denver and the area. Today Denver is the largest city and the capital of Colorado. Locate Denver on the map on pages 208 – 209.

Why do you think people might like to visit Miami Beach?

world visit Miami Beach. They like the white sandy beaches, the big hotels, the stores, and places to eat. Climate has helped Miami Beach become a big city.

Atlanta Not all cities owe their growth to natural resources. Some cities have grown up where important train lines or highways meet. Atlanta, Georgia, is such a city.

Atlanta began as a small railroad town. For years, trains carried products to and from Atlanta. When highways were

Trains were important to Atlanta's growth.

Miami Beach There is still another natural resource that has helped some cities grow. That is **climate.** Climate is the kind of **weather** that a place has all year. Weather is made up of rainfall, snowfall, wind, and **temperature.** The temperature is how hot or cold it is in a place.

The state of Florida has a warm climate. Miami Beach is a city in Florida. Many people have moved there to enjoy the warm winters. Others have moved to Miami Beach to work in businesses that serve visitors to the area. People from all over the

This is a picture of Atlanta today. Compare the buildings and roads with those shown in the picture at the bottom of page 74.

built, trucks began to carry products, too. Now Atlanta has become a major transportation center for the southeastern United States. Atlanta is also the largest city and the capital of Georgia. Find Atlanta on the map on pages 208 — 209.

Washington, D.C. Some cities begin and grow for still another reason. Our nation's capital is Washington, D.C. It began as a planned city. The leaders of our country wanted a special city that would serve as the home of our nation's government. The capital city was built on land given to the nation by the state of Maryland.

Washington, D.C., is called a **government city**. Many of the laws and plans for all the people in the United States are made in Washington. It takes many people to make those laws and plans. You will read more about Washington, D.C., in Chapter 7.

CHECKUP

1. How did farming change the way people lived long ago?
2. Name at least four reasons why cities began and grew.
3. What is a natural resource?

People Live and Work in Cities

Where do people live? All people need a home, or shelter. Our homes protect us from the weather. They also give us a safe place to live.

There are several kinds of homes in large cities. Some people live in tall buildings where other people live. These buildings sometimes have a hundred or more families living in them. A single person or a family lives in a group of rooms called an **apartment.** Apartment buildings are homes for many people.

Other people live in single houses. Usually only one family lives in each single house. Some single houses have a yard around them. Others may be joined

These beautiful houses were built many years ago in San Francisco. They have been well cared for by the people who live in them.

These single houses in Stamford, Connecticut, have yards around them. In the background you can see some tall apartment buildings. There are many apartments in each building.

together to make a row of houses. The pictures on these pages show some apartment buildings and single houses in different cities.

These kinds of homes may be found in smaller communities, too. But in cities the apartment buildings are often much larger. Single houses in cities are often much closer together than they are in small towns.

Where do people work? Cities need many workers. Some workers make products such as clothes, shoes, tools, and radios. They work in buildings that are called **factories.** Factories have machines that help these workers make the products. Some factories are very large. Two or three thousand people may work in one factory.

A visit to a factory There are several automobile factories in Detroit, Michigan. Detroit is often called the "Automobile Capital of the World." More automobiles are made in and near Detroit than anywhere else in the world. Look at the map on pages 208 – 209 and find Detroit.

The men and women who work in factories have many different jobs. Let us visit a factory and see how the people work together.

We are going to visit just one part of an automobile factory. It is called the **assembly line.** This is where the new cars are put together, or assembled. The cars are pulled along the assembly line by machine. There are many workers on the assembly line. Each worker has a different job to do in assembling the car. The assembly line puts cars together fast.

This large factory has three assembly lines. On one line the body of the car is put together. Here the floor, roof, and sides of the car are joined or welded together. Next the body is

ASSEMBLING THE BODY

Welding the roof

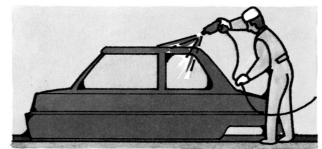
Painting the body

Putting in window glass

painted. After it is painted, the inside of the car is finished. The windows and seats are then placed in the car. At this point, this assembly line meets another assembly line.

The second line carries the frame of the car. This frame holds the car together. The motor is placed on the frame and the tires are attached.

ASSEMBLING THE FRAME

Adding the front suspension

Putting the motor in

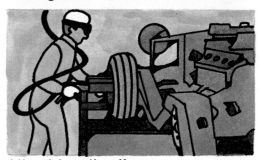

Attaching the tires

FINAL ASSEMBLY

Joining the body to the frame

Adding the front end

Water-testing the car

The drawings above show some of the important steps in assembling an automobile.

On the final assembly line, the frame and the body are joined together. The car is checked to be sure that it is assembled correctly. It is even water-tested to see if it has any leaks. After these tests, someone starts the engine and drives the car off the assembly line.

Now the car is ready to be sold. It will be shipped from the factory to a car dealer. The car dealer may be in the same city, another American city, or in a foreign country. People who want to buy a new car will go to a car dealer. Many new cars are sold every year.

Buying and selling goods A car is just one product you may buy in a city. There are thousands of other **goods** for sale. You can find just about anything you might want to buy in city stores.

Some stores are small. They are owned by one or two people who work in them. A small store usually sells only a few kinds of products. Other stores, such as department stores, are large. They have hundreds of different goods for sale. You can buy clothes, shoes, toys, and even furniture in a department store. Large stores need many workers.

This is an outdoor market in Philadelphia, Pennsylvania. What products are people buying and selling?

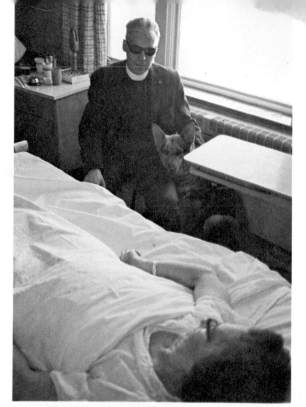

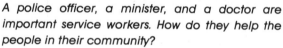
A police officer, a minister, and a doctor are important service workers. How do they help the people in their community?

Giving service You have learned that people in cities make, buy, and sell goods. People also provide **services.** A service is a kind of work that helps people. A doctor helps people who are sick. A teacher helps children learn. A barber helps people by cutting their hair. These people are paid for their services. They use the money they earn for their services to buy the goods they need. Look at the pictures on this page. What kinds of services are these people doing?

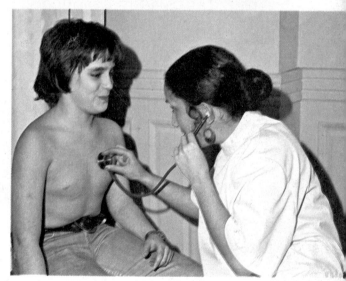

CHECKUP

1. How is an apartment building different from a single house?
2. Explain how a car is put together on an assembly line.
3. What kinds of work do people in cities do?
4. What is service work?

People Have Fun in Cities

Many things to do   People live and work in cities, but they also have fun. Large cities have many interesting places to visit and things to do. Let us meet some students who live in five large American cities. These students will tell you about some of the things they enjoy doing where they live.

Jeff's city   Jeff lives in Miami, Florida. Find the city on the map on pages 208–209.

"Miami is a great place to live," says Jeff. "The weather is almost always warm. We don't have cold winters like some other cities. It hardly ever snows in Miami.

"On weekends, I like to swim in the ocean at Miami Beach. This city is just a few miles from Miami. The beaches are usually crowded with visitors.

"In March, I always go with my family to see some spring-training baseball games. Many teams come

At the Seaquarium in Miami, the dolphins perform tricks in the water show.

to Florida to practice because the weather is too cold in their own cities.

"One of my favorite places is the Seaquarium, where you can see all kinds of sea animals. There is a killer-whale show with two stars. They are Lolita and Hugo. Together they weigh over 16,000 pounds (7,260 kg). I have seen a man ride on Lolita. He even put his head in her mouth.

"Every time I go to the Seaquarium, I see the show with Flipper. Flipper is the only dolphin that has starred in a television series."

Maria's city   Maria lives in San Antonio, Texas. She will tell you about her home city. Look at the map of the United States on pages 208–209. Can you find San Antonio?

"My favorite place in the whole city is the area called the Paseo del Rio (pä sä' ō del rē' ō)," says Maria. "This is where the San Antonio River runs through the **business center**, or main part, of the city. At night and on weekends, I love to walk along the river with my family. There are many stores and places to eat. There are boats that float along the river at night. You can eat supper on these boats.

"I think the best time of year in San Antonio is April. For ten days there is a fiesta (fē es' tə), or big celebration. The fiesta ends with a parade on the river. Boats are decorated and the parade is held at night. Last year, I dressed in a costume and rode on one of the boats. I had a wonderful time waving at the people who were watching from the shore."

The Paseo del Rio in San Antonio borders the San Antonio River. In English, Paseo del Rio means "river walk."

Discover the secrets of Movie Magic!

4. The MCA Tower. You've seen it in hundreds of movies and TV shows.

5. Front Lot. Look around you. Over 34 movie and TV stages, editorial, wardrobe, make-up, sound, casting, music recording, stars' dressing rooms, and other vital production facilities.

6. Sound Stage. Visitors chosen for "bionic" training leap over impossible heights just like the SIX-MILLION-DOLLAR MAN and BIONIC WOMAN. Lift a 3,000-lb. truck and run 60 mph. Learn about special effects.

7. The Battle of Galactica.™ The Tour's most elaborate special effect. Get caught in a spectacular laser battle between evil aliens and a courageous Colonial warrior.

8. Collapsing Bridge. One of the Tour's most startling special effects. Will you make it across OK?

9. Burning House. The leaping flames and billowing smoke are absolutely "reel."

10. The Doomed Glacier Avalanche. Into an icy chasm — suddenly you are plunged over the edge into an Alpine avalanche.

11. Prop Plaza. When the tram stops here, you'll find refreshments, stores and the most amazing movie props ever devised, waiting for you to photograph.

12. Mexican Village. Can be seen in the CBS TV series, "The Incredible Hulk."

13. Flash Flood. It happens right before your eyes.

14. "Psycho" House. From Alfred Hitchcock's classic scary movie. Don't get too close!

15. Six Points. These Western sets have played host to Hollywood's most famous cowboys, from Tom Mix to John Wayne.

16. Torpedo Run. Watch this explosive bit of Hollywood trickery used in ABC's "Operation Petticoat."

17. Red Sea. A most astounding movie miracle. It parts daily...right next to a famous stone bridge in "New York's Central Park."

18. Runaway Train. It looks so real, but the danger's all fun. Isn't it?

19. "JAWS." The deadly 24-foot shark from "Jaws" returns to attack your tram — and you.

*BIONIC WOMAN, JAWS, SIX-MILLION-DOLLAR MAN, BIONIC and UNIVERSAL STUDIOS TOUR are trademarks of Universal City Studios, Inc.
©1980 Universal City Studios, Inc.

1. Tour Entrance. Information and Visitor Center. Where it all begins!

2. Entertainment Center.
CASTLE DRACULA: At our newest and most terrifying attraction, you'll encounter Count Dracula and his menagerie of classic Universal monsters, bats and wolves.
THE ANIMAL SHOW: You'll see animal movie stars perform incredible tricks just like they do in the movies.
THE STUNT SHOW: An exhibition of bone-jarring fights where some of Hollywood's most daring stunt men actually fall off buildings and sink into quicksand.
AIRPORT SCREEN TEST THEATRE: Where you'll experience the movie crash and rescue scenes in front of real videotape cameras. And then see yourself on the screen within minutes.
FOOD & SHOPS: Delicious refreshments and unusual gifts.

3. Universal Amphitheatre.® Where the stars come out at night — an acoustically perfect pop music showcase.

Which places would you like to see at Universal Studios?

The person falling from a building is doing a stunt for a movie.

Nicholas's city   Nicholas lives in Los Angeles, California. It is the largest city in the state. Find Los Angeles on page 208.

Nicholas tells about his two favorite places. "One of these places is the beach. We have miles of beaches along the Pacific Ocean. You can always find people there on weekends and in the summer.

"The other place is Universal Studios. The people who work there make movies and television shows. You can ride on a train that takes you all around the streets of the studio. You ride past houses and buildings, but they are not real. They only have fronts. They do not have backs or roofs. But in the movies they look real."

Cindy's city   Cindy lives in Chicago, Illinois. Locate Chicago on the map on pages 208 — 209.

Cindy says, "In the summer I go sailing on Lake Michigan with my parents. We have a small sailboat. Sometimes I sail it with their help.

"We keep our boat in the water by Grant Park. When we sail back to the city at the end of the day, it seems as if we are sailing right into the middle of the city. It is beautiful late in the afternoon. You can see the sun set behind the tall buildings."

The Sears Tower in Chicago is the world's tallest building.

The Statue of Liberty stands on Liberty Island in New York Harbor.

Frank's city   Frank lives in New York City. Find the city on the map on pages 208 — 209.

"There are always things to do in New York City," explains Frank. "I like to go to basketball games with my uncle. And my brothers take me to see the circus when it comes to Madison Square Garden. But my favorite place is the American Museum of Natural History. It is a big place with many things to see. I especially like to look at the stuffed animals. They look like they are alive.

"Last summer my cousins came to visit us. We took them shopping in the department stores. We also took them to the top of the World Trade Center. It is an office building that is 110 stories high. From the top, we could see for miles.

"The best trip was our ride on the ferryboat to Liberty Island. We went there to see the Statue of Liberty. The statue was given to the people of the United States by the people of France. It has become a symbol of our country's freedom."

You have read about the things these five girls and boys like to do in and around their home city. Each one enjoys something different. What are some things you especially like to do in your community?

CHECKUP

1. Name at least seven different things the students like to do in their city.
2. In which state is San Antonio located? Where is Chicago located?

86

Cities Need Transportation

Moving people and products

People travel for a variety of reasons. They go to school, to work, to the store, and to many other places. They need some ways to move about their city or town. People also need some ways to move goods from one place to another. Transportation meets these needs.

There are three kinds of transportation. People and goods can be moved by land, water, or air. Cars, buses, trucks, and trains provide transportation on land. Ships move people and goods by water, while airplanes move them by air. Today people and goods travel to almost every part of the earth.

Throughout the world, millions of people travel on trains each day.

Trains Usually trains carry the biggest or heaviest products. The products are carried in different kinds of railroad cars. One kind is called a boxcar. It has closed sides, a roof, and sliding doors. Boxcars carry many products, such as drinking glasses from Charleston, West Virginia, and typewriters from Hartford, Connecticut. Boxcars also carry **wheat** from places such as Bismarck, North Dakota. The wheat will be made into flour and used to make bread.

Another railroad car is a refrigerator car. These cars carry products such as meat from Chicago, Illinois, and fresh fruit from Indian River, Florida. A refrigerator car keeps the meat and fruit cold.

Another railroad car is called a flatcar. It does not have sides or ends. It has only a floor. Flatcars often carry new automobiles and trucks from factories in and near Detroit, Michigan.

Trains often carry new automobiles.

A tank car has a roof and rounded sides. It carries different kinds of liquids. Tank cars may carry oil from Philadelphia, Pennsylvania, or chemicals from Wilmington, Delaware.

Railroads touch all parts of our country. They bring us many of the goods we need and want. They also provide transportation for many people. Passenger trains travel between hundreds of cities in the United States.

Trucks   Trucks are used to move things by land. They bring us many different products. Trucks are the most common way of moving products. Sometime you might want to count the number of trucks you see in one day. You will probably see many more trucks than trains or airplanes.

Trucks can carry almost anything. They bring oranges from Florida or California, and furniture from North Carolina. They also bring bread from the bakeries, milk from the dairies, and wood from the lumber mills.

Airplanes   Airplanes move people and products very quickly. The place where airplanes land and take off is called an **airport.** All of our biggest cities have very large airports. Thousands of airplanes land and take off from these airports every day.

A visit to an airport   You met some students from Alfred Vail School in Chapter 2. We are going to follow Mrs. Reilly and her class as they visit a large airport about 20 miles (32 km) from Morristown. This is the Newark International Airport. Look at the map on pages 208 – 209. Can you find Newark, New Jersey?

Mr. Chou met the school bus. He took the class on a tour of the airport. They even went inside an airplane. When their visit was over, Mr. Chou gave the students some pictures. He hoped the pictures would help them remember what they had learned about the airport. You can see the pictures on page 90.

At the airport, passengers buy tickets to ride on the airplanes. The people who sell the tickets are called ticket agents.

Before getting on an airplane, passengers must walk through a special machine. The machine can tell if a passenger is carrying a metal weapon.

A big sign tells passengers when airplanes are landing, or arriving. The sign also tells when airplanes are taking off, or departing.

FLIGHT	ARRIVE	DEPART	AREA	REMARKS
	79	10:55	79	
10		11:00	80	NEW YORK CITY
899	11:00		76	
510	10:50	11:15	73	
76		11:20	75	
232		11:20	81	SEATTLE/TACOMA
51	11:30		83	BALTIMORE
2106		11:35	70	CHICAGO

Suitcases and packages have tags put on them. The tags tell where the suitcases and packages are going. Then they are placed on the right airplane.

Ships   Very large and heavy products are often moved by water. Many of our largest cities have busy ports. Ports are places where products are loaded or unloaded from ships. Look at the map of the United States on pages 208 — 209. Notice how many large cities are found along oceans, lakes, and rivers.

Whenever we think about transportation by water, we usually think of huge ships that sail the seas. There are different kinds of ships. **Cargo ships** carry many different products, or cargo. These products are usually packed in giant-sized boxes called containers. The containers are unloaded by huge cranes. These machines lift the containers off the ship and onto the ground. Once on the ground, the containers are loaded on trucks and taken to stores.

Another kind of ship is a **tanker.** Tankers have huge tanks in which they carry oil or other kinds of liquid. Pumps and pipes are used to unload these ships.

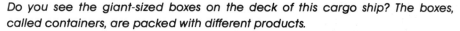

Do you see the giant-sized boxes on the deck of this cargo ship? The boxes, called containers, are packed with different products.

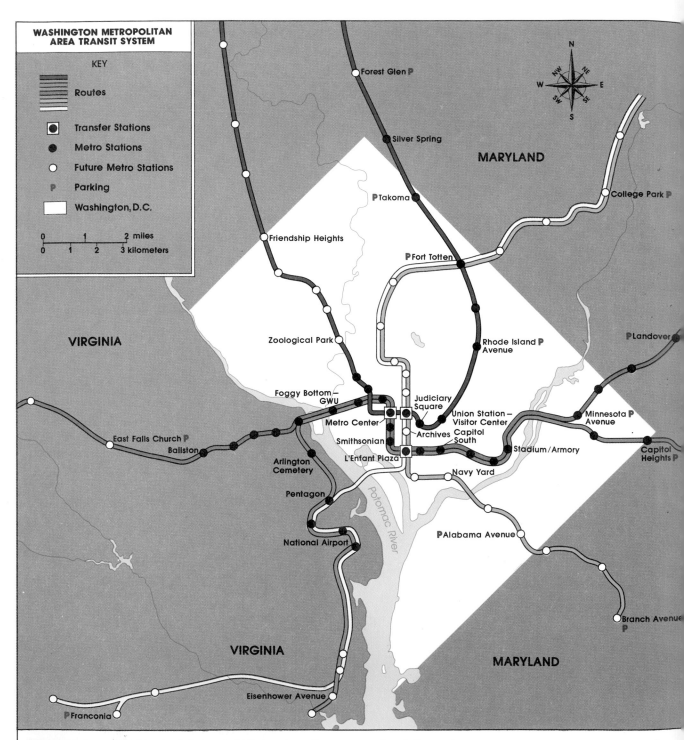

WASHINGTON METROPOLITAN AREA TRANSIT SYSTEM

KEY

Routes

■ Transfer Stations

● Metro Stations

○ Future Metro Stations

P Parking

□ Washington, D.C.

```
0        1         2 miles
0    1    2    3 kilometers
```

MARYLAND

VIRGINIA

VIRGINIA

MARYLAND

Forest Glen P

Silver Spring

P Takoma

College Park P

P Fort Totten

Friendship Heights

Zoological Park

Rhode Island P
Avenue

P Landover

Foggy Bottom—
GWU

Judiciary
Square

Union Station—
Visitor Center

Minnesota P
Avenue

East Falls Church P

Ballston

Metro Center

Archives

Capitol
South

Smithsonian

Stadium/Armory

Capitol
Heights P

Arlington
Cemetery

L'Enfant Plaza

Navy Yard

Pentagon

P Alabama Avenue

National Airport

Branch Avenue
P

Eisenhower Avenue

P Franconia

Potomac River

This map shows Washington's transportation system. You can see the stations where
the trains stop and the routes the trains follow.

92

Many people travel around a city on subway trains.

Getting around in a city   So far you have learned mostly about transportation *between* cities. How do people get around *in* cities?

People in cities go from place to place in different ways. Sometimes they walk. Sometimes they ride on a **subway.** A subway is a train that runs under the ground. Some people ride in their car or truck. Others ride in a bus or **taxicab.** A taxicab is a car for hire. You must pay the taxi driver to take you where you want to go. A few people even ride bicycles on busy city streets.

How cities change   Cities are always changing. Some changes take place because cities grow. As more and more people move to cities, new homes and buildings are built. New roads are built to help people travel to places in their community.

Cities have also changed because of new ways of doing things. Years ago, there were no airports because there were no airplanes. There were no large highways because there were few cars. Today there are airports and highways to serve the transportation needs of our cities.

CHECKUP

1. Name the three kinds of transportation.
2. What is the difference between a cargo ship and a tanker?
3. Name at least five ways that people go from place to place within a city.

3 / CHAPTER REVIEW

KEY FACTS

1. The first cities began when people learned to grow more than enough food for their own needs.

2. Natural resources, such as rich farmland, water, and climate, helped many cities begin and grow.

3. People in cities live mostly in apartment buildings and single houses.

4. In large cities, many people work in factories and stores. Other people work by providing services.

5. The three kinds of transportation are air, land, and water.

VOCABULARY QUIZ

Write the numbers 1 to 5 on a sheet of paper. Read each sentence below. The underlined words are vocabulary words. Write **T** if the sentence is true and **F** if it is false.

1. Climate is the kind of weather a place has all year.

2. A tanker is a ship that carries boxes or containers.

3. A factory is a place of work where machines are used to make products.

4. Transportation is the means by which people and products move from place to place.

5. A valley is a lowland between hills or mountains.

REVIEW QUESTIONS

1. Why did each of the following communities grow to be a large city? **(a)** Cincinnati **(b)** Denver **(c)** Atlanta

2. List some jobs that service workers might do in a community.

3. What are some of the things that people living in cities do for fun?

4. Why do cities need transportation?

5. What are some of the things you might see if you visited an airport?

ACTIVITY

Choose one of these cities to learn more about.

1. Rio de Janeiro, Brazil
2. London, England
3. Tokyo, Japan
4. Mexico City, Mexico
5. Montreal, Canada
6. Tel Aviv, Israel
7. Cairo, Egypt
8. Nairobi, Kenya
9. Paris, France

Write a report about the city. Use encyclopedias or other books for information. Some things to include in your report are
- name of the city and country
- products made in the city
- kinds of transportation
- kinds of homes

READING A SCHEDULE

USING A BASEBALL SCHEDULE

Most of our largest cities have major league baseball teams. When spring training ends, the teams go back to their home cities. There the teams play baseball from April to October.

At the beginning of each season, the teams publish schedules. The schedules show information about the games. Below is part of a schedule for the San Francisco Giants.

This schedule shows the games the Giants will play in August. It tells whether the game will be played at home in San Francisco or away in the other team's city. It tells which team the Giants will play and what time the game begins. The name of each team is shortened on the schedule, but you can see what the abbreviation stands for below the schedule. For example, ATL. is the abbreviation for the Atlanta Braves. The schedule also shows other kinds of information.

SKILLS PRACTICE

Read the schedule and answer the questions below. Write your answers on a separate sheet of paper.

1. How many days do the Giants play at home in August?
2. Which team do the Giants play on August 21?
3. On which day do the Giants play a doubleheader?
4. When does the doubleheader begin?
5. In which city is the game played on August 31?

■ Home Games		**Giants Schedule**			☐ Away Games	
			August			
SUN.	MON.	TUES.	WED.	THURS.	FRI.	SAT.
● 1 HOU.	● 2 ATL.	● 3 ATL.	● 4 ATL.	● 5 HOU.	● 6 HOU.	○ 7 HOU.
○ DH 8 HOU.	● 9 ATL.	● 10 ATL.	○ 11 ATL.	○ 12 L.A.	● 13 L.A.	● 14 L.A.
○ 15 L.A.	16	● 17 PIT.	● 18 PIT.	● 19 PIT.	● 20 ST.L.	● 21 ST.L.
○ 22 ST.L.	○ 23 CHI.	○ 24 CHI.	○ 25 CHI.	26	● 27 PIT.	○ 28 PIT.
○ 29 PIT.	30	● 31 CHI.				

ATL. —Atlanta Braves
CHI. —Chicago Cubs
HOU. —Houston Astros
L.A. —Los Angeles Dodgers
ST.L. —St. Louis Cardinals
PIT. —Pittsburgh Pirates

○ Day Games 1:05 P.M.
● Night Games 7:35 P.M.
DH Doubleheaders 12:05 P.M.

CHAPTER

4 Living in Smaller Communities

People Live and Work in a Small Town

┌─VOCABULARY─────────────────┐
│ suburb   housing   │
│ sawmill   development   │
└──────────────────────────────┘

Towns across the country
In the last chapter you learned about large cities. In this chapter you will learn about smaller communities called towns. There are many towns in the United States. Some towns are in the mountains. Some are located along rivers or near oceans. Other towns are near farmlands. Many Americans live and work in towns across the country.

The author of this book lives in a small town named Humble. Humble is in southeastern Texas. It is located just a few miles from Houston. Look at the map on pages 208–209 and find the city of Houston.

Houston is the largest city in Texas. Humble is a **suburb** of Houston. Communities near large cities are called suburbs.

How a town got its name
The town of Humble was named for a man named Pleasant Humble. He lived in the area more than a hundred years ago. Mr. Humble ran a ferryboat on the nearby San Jacinto (san jə sint′ ō) River. The river supplied the early settlers with fish and water.

Mr. Humble also set up a post office. He helped deliver mail to people who lived around him. Soon all letters for people who lived in the area were sent to Mr. Humble. In time, Mr. Humble's name was taken for the name of the town.

Many other communities in the United States have been named after people. How did your community get its name?

This photograph shows a suburb in central Massachusetts.

Trains carried pine and oak trees from the forest to the sawmills in and near Humble.

Natural resources You have read in Chapter 3 how natural resources helped some cities grow. Natural resources also helped smaller communities grow.

The area that became Humble was in the middle of a forest. Many large pine and oak trees grew there.

Some of the first settlers in the area built **sawmills.** The machines in the sawmills cut the trees into boards. The boards were used to build homes, stores, and other buildings. Soon train lines were built to carry the wood from Humble to other communities.

In 1904 oil was discovered near Humble. Soon after the first oil well was drilled, oil companies moved to Houston. They wanted to be near the oil fields. More and more wells were drilled. Some of the older residents of Humble say they remember walking to school without touching the ground. They say that the oil wells were so close together they could just jump from one well to another.

Oil fields were opened up quickly after oil was discovered near Humble.

Growth of a town   At first most of the workers in the oil fields and the owners of the oil wells lived in Houston. They took a train to Humble every morning. They went back to Houston every night because there was no place to live in Humble. Then some of the workers put up small tents near the oil wells.

The tents had no water, so a woman named Mrs. Lambrecht dug a water well. She built a bathhouse. The workers and their families used the bathhouse and the water to bathe and wash clothes. The bathhouse is no longer there, but the water well still flows today.

Mrs. Lambrecht's water well marks the place where the bathhouse once stood.

This is part of the downtown business district in Humble.

Humble has changed since the days of the first oil wells. The town has grown from 75 people in the 1890s to 6,700 people in the 1980s. It is no longer an oil town. Many of the wells were closed after most of the oil near the surface was pumped out.

Humble has continued to grow without the oil wells. As you have read, Humble is a suburb of a very large city—Houston. As Houston has grown, so have its suburbs. More and more people are moving to Humble.

99

Where do people live? Like many other small towns in the United States, Humble has some apartment buildings. The tallest building is four stories high. Some townspeople live in these apartments.

Many other townspeople live in single houses. Some of the single houses in Humble are more than 50 years old, but most of them are much newer. These newer houses are often built in **housing developments.** A housing development is a group of homes that is planned by a builder. The builder buys land and divides it into many lots, or small pieces of ground. On each lot, the builder puts up a house and then sells it. In Humble, housing developments now cover hundreds of acres of land.

Where do people work? People who live in the suburbs often work in the nearby city. Some people from Humble work in the stores and office buildings in Houston.

Other people work at the Houston Intercontinental Airport. The airport is just a few miles from Humble. The airport and the airline companies need many different workers. Some people from Humble are pilots. They fly the airplanes. Others have jobs selling airplane tickets. Some people are mechanics who repair the airplanes. Can you think of any other jobs needed to run an airport? Would you like to work at an airport?

A number of people in Humble work in the town. Years ago, there were few stores in Humble.

This shopping center in Humble has a variety of stores.

At the right in this picture is a special ladder truck. The long boom has a built-in hose that shoots water at a fire.

Today, there are many stores and businesses. Humble has office buildings and several modern shopping centers. It also has a hospital, a library, and a museum. It has banks, schools, and places of worship. It has offices for doctors and dentists. There are jobs for people at each of these places.

Volunteer firefighters There is a special group of workers in Humble. They are the members of the volunteer fire department. In some small towns, such as Humble, the community cannot afford to pay their firefighters. So the people volunteer, or give, their time to help put out fires. They go to school to learn about their jobs. They also spend hours keeping the fire trucks and hoses in good condition.

Whenever there is a fire, the firefighters are called at their homes or places of work. They go to the fire either on the fire truck or in their own cars. As they drive to the fire, firefighters use sirens and flashing red and blue lights. The lights and sirens let people know that the firefighters must get to the fire quickly. People drive their cars to the side of the road to let the fire trucks pass.

Not all towns have a volunteer fire department. Some have a full-time fire department. These firefighters are paid by their community for their work. Large cities such as Houston, Texas, or Los Angeles, California, have hundreds of full-time firefighters.

CHECKUP

1. What is a suburb?
2. Which natural resources were important to Humble's growth as a community?
3. How is a volunteer fire department different from a full-time fire department?

Community Events

Why are small towns special?
Towns and cities are alike in many ways. They all have homes and places of business. They have streets and schools and places of worship. The main difference between towns and cities is size. Towns have fewer people. They also have fewer buildings and businesses.

Some towns are very small. If your family has lived in such a town for a long time, you may know almost everyone else there. When people have known other families for many years, they usually feel close to one another.

People in small towns often feel proud of their community because they feel they are an important part of it. Most people know the leaders of their community. Some leaders might have grown up in the town. Who are leaders in your community?

Many families like to get together for picnics.

Celebrating the Fourth of July

People around the world enjoy celebrating holidays. A favorite holiday in many American cities and towns is on July 4. This is **Independence Day.** On this day more than 200 years ago, the United States became a free nation. Each year, Americans celebrate their nation's birthday with flags, music, and parades.

In the community of Humble, Independence Day is a time for people to get together for picnics and cookouts. A cookout is sometimes called a **barbecue.** At a barbecue, meat is roasted over hot coals. Some people add the wood from a mesquite (mes kēt′) tree to the fire. They say that the smoke from the mesquite gives meat a real Texas flavor.

At night after the picnics and barbecues end, there is a big fireworks display. It is held at the high school football stadium. Many townspeople go to see the beautiful fireworks each year. Some of the fireworks are shot so high into the sky that people all over town can see them from their own backyards.

How do you celebrate Independence Day in your community?

The Humble Hornet

PARK AND RIDE
by Marcia West

   Many people are parking their cars and riding a bus to work. They park their cars at the Kingwood Church on Woodland Hills Road. A bus takes them to Houston. The city is 23 miles away.

   The people who ride the bus say that it saves them time and money. The buses have been so popular that more buses are going to be used starting on May 6.

NEW FIRE TRUCK
by Manuel Mendez

   We have a new fire truck in our community. It is big and red.

   The truck was first used at a grass fire on Black Cat Ridge. The big horn at the fire station blew. Then volunteer fire fighters ran to the station. They rode to the fire on the new truck. Then they put out the fire.

LITTLE LEAGUE
by Betsy McKenna

   Tryouts for Little League teams will start on Saturday, April 18. The tryouts will begin at 9 A.M. They will be held on the field behind Humble Elementary School.

SHOPPING MALL
by Eddie Brown

   A new shopping center is going to be built in Humble. The mall will be built between Farm and Market Roads along U.S. Highway 59. It will be called Deerbrook Mall.

   There will be more than 40 stores in the mall. The stores will be all in a group under one roof.

ALICE IN WONDERLAND
by Steve DeLorenzo

   The fourth grade will put on a play on May 1 and May 2. The play is Alice in Wonderland. It will be put on three times. The first time will be at 10 A.M. on Friday, May 1. The other times will be Friday and Saturday, May 2, at 7 P.M. All shows will be in the school auditorium.

   Tickets can be bought at the door. They can also be bought at the bank or from any member of the P.T.A.

FEED STORE GROWS
by Lucy Levy

   The Humble Feed Store has grown. It has all kinds of feed, or food, for animals. Mr. Sanders owns the store. He said he needed more room so he made the store larger.

   The Feed Store is also the bus station. Buses from Houston and other cities stop at the store.

104

Writing a newspaper In Humble, Independence Day is a big event. There are also many other things happening in the community. Some students in Humble have written a school newspaper. It tells about some of the things that are taking place in their town. As you read their newspaper on page 104, think about the many things that are happening in your community.

1. How are cities and towns alike?
2. What is the main difference between large cities and small towns?
3. Why do people in the United States celebrate Independence Day?

People Have Fun in Towns

VOCABULARY

trail ride	blacksmith
trail boss	

Many things to do You have read in Chapter 3 about the interesting places to visit and things to do in cities. People living in towns enjoy doing many of the same things. They like to visit parks and museums. They play baseball and ride bicycles. Sometimes they go into a nearby city and spend a day shopping or seeing the circus.

A parade is one way to celebrate a holiday in many American communities.

A trail ride　　Many people in Humble like to ride horses. Most of the horses are kept at stables. A stable has several barns. The horses live in the barns. Workers at the stables feed and care for the horses. The owners of the horses go to the stables and ride their horses through fields.

Every year some of these people ride their horses in the Salt Grass Trail Ride. A **trail ride** is a trip on horseback along a planned route. More than 1,100 people go on the Salt Grass Trail Ride every year. Most of the riders are from Texas and other states. Some riders, however, are from Mexico and Canada.

The riders meet on Sunday in Cat Spring, Texas. They travel from there into the center of Houston. This is a distance of about 50 miles (80 km). It takes the riders six days to ride this far on their horses.

The Salt Grass Trail Ride is one of six trail rides that take place every year before the exciting Houston Livestock Show and Rodeo (rō′ dē ō). You will read about the Livestock Show and Rodeo in Chapter 5. Each of the six trail rides comes to Houston from a different direction.

The **trail boss** for the Salt Grass Trail Ride is named Gene Beckendorff. He has an important job. He has to choose campsites. These are the places for the riders to camp and spend the night. He must be sure there is plenty of food. He must also be sure the riders travel far enough each day.

Mr. Beckendorff tells about the Salt Grass Trail Ride. "Each day we are up before the sun rises. The food cooking over the

Meet Gene Beckendorff. He is the trail boss for the Salt Grass Trail Ride.

campfires and on the stoves smells so good in the morning.

"We load the wagons, saddle the horses, and start the ride. We ride along the roads. The metal shoes on the horses protect them from the hard roads. Sometimes, though, a horse will lose a shoe. Then it is the job of the **blacksmith** to put a new shoe on the horse. The blacksmith travels with us on the trail ride.

"In the middle of the day, we stop for lunch. Vans have been sent ahead to fix lunch for some of us. Other riders make lunch when we stop.

The blacksmith trims the horse's hoof to fit the metal horseshoe.

The riders come from many states as well as from Mexico and Canada. The trail ride travels from Cat Spring, Texas, into the center of Houston.

The big dance at Bear Creek Park is fun for everyone on the Salt Grass Trail Ride.

Many people come out to see the trail riders as they pass by.

At the end of a long day, the riders take it easy around a campfire. Some people camp out in tents while others sleep in campers and trucks.

"At night we camp out. Some riders put up tents. Others sleep in trucks and campers. We all eat outside. Food cooked over a fire always seems to taste better.

"Our last two nights on the trail are the most fun. We ride to Bear Creek Park on Wednesday afternoon. The park is about 15 miles (24 km) from downtown Houston. There is always a big dance at Bear Creek Park. Even people from Houston come to the dance.

"The next day we ride into Houston. As we pass by schools, students come out to see us. It is not every day that they see so many horses and wagons on a busy highway.

"We spend Thursday night in Memorial Park. There we meet riders from five other trail rides. Almost 6,000 trail riders spend the night in Memorial Park.

"The next morning we saddle up and ride into downtown Houston. Bands and floats join

us for the rodeo parade. Schools are usually closed. This lets everyone see the parade. We all enjoy the parade, but it seems funny to ride horses between the huge buildings.

"The trail ride ends after the parade. Some riders stay in Houston for the Livestock Show and Rodeo. Others load their horses into vans and drive home. Everyone has made many new friends on the trail ride."

After five days of travel by horse and wagon, the riders reach the end of the trail in Houston.

CHECKUP

1. What does the trail boss do on the trail ride?
2. Why is a blacksmith important to have along on the trail ride?

Crowds line the streets of downtown Houston to see the rodeo parade.

Transportation from the Suburbs to the City

Commuter problems You know that some of the people who live in Humble work in Houston. These people are called **commuters** (kə myü′ tərz). They commute, or travel regularly, back and forth from their homes in the suburbs to their work in the city. Commuters may drive their cars to work. They may ride in buses or share cars with other people. Many people use the same roads and highways.

What happens when many of these people try to drive on the roads at about the same time? If you have ever been to a football game, you know what happens. Everyone tries to leave when the game is over. The cars cannot all fit on the road at the same time. You may sit awhile in your car before you leave the parking lot. Once you are on the road, the cars move slowly.

There is usually heavy traffic on the highways of southern California.

The same thing happens in Houston during the **rush hour**. This is the time of day when most people are going to work or coming home from work. The streets of Houston become very crowded with cars, trucks, buses, and taxicabs. **Traffic** moves very slowly. It may take commuters a long time to travel to and from the city each day.

Traffic jams and long traveling times are two of the problems that face commuters. Another problem is the amount of gasoline that commuters use to drive to work.

A gasoline shortage in 1979 caused long lines to form at many gas stations.

Gasoline is a product made from oil. There is a great need to use oil wisely. We cannot afford to waste this valuable natural resource. If we do waste it now, the world may soon run out of oil. To help solve this problem, people in communities across the country are looking for ways to save on gas.

What can people do? Some people in Morristown, New Jersey, are interested in solving the problem. Mrs. Reilly and some of her students talked about ways to save gasoline.

Mrs. Reilly: We have all seen higher prices for gasoline. We have seen long lines of cars at gas stations. We have even seen stations run out of gas to sell. What are some things people can do to help save gasoline?

Joyce: Mom and Dad are always talking about how much gas costs. They said that they are trying to drive less. One thing they told me was that we can't drive to the store every time we want to. We are trying to do most of our shopping in one trip.

Mrs. Reilly: Joyce, how does your family do the shopping in one trip?

Joyce: Well, last Friday night Mom and Dad gave me a map of Morristown. They also gave me a list of places that we needed to go to on Saturday. We sat down and planned our trip so that we would travel the shortest route.

Howard: When we need one or two things from the store, we ride our bikes. My father has even bought a bike. He rides it to his office here in town.

Mrs. Reilly: I know some of your parents commute to work every day. In what ways are they saving gas as they travel?

Maria: My father works in New York City. He used to drive there every day. Now he takes the train. He says that the train costs him less money. He doesn't have to worry about parking the car in the city or about traffic jams and accidents, either.

Bill: My mother rides to work with other people. She takes our car only once a week. She works at the same place as Gabe's father and some other people who live close to us.

Gabe: My father calls this car pooling. There are five people in the **car pool.** Each person in the car pool drives one day a week. This saves a lot of gas because they are using only one car instead of five cars.

Betty: My father rides to work with other people, too. He works in Newark, New Jersey. His company bought some vans. They are used by company workers who ride together. My father drives one of the vans. On work days, he picks up nine other people who work for his company. Then he drives them to work. My father calls this a van pool.

The students in Mrs. Reilly's class had all heard about some ways to save gas. Do you know any different ways?

These people ride to work each day in van pools. The vans are parked in a special area.

Commuting to San Francisco

You have read how people in Humble commute into Houston. You have also read how people in Morristown commute into New York City. Now let us look at how commuters travel to and from the city of San Francisco.

San Francisco is located in California. Find the city on the map of the United States on pages 208–209. Is San Francisco located in the mountains or on the coast?

Many people who live near San Francisco drive their cars into the city. There are two bridges leading into the city. Each day thousands of cars cross these bridges.

Can you think of another way people might travel to the city? San Francisco has water almost all the way around it. Some people travel into the city on a boat. This boat is called a ferry. Ferries carry hundreds of people to San Francisco every day. Ferries also carry cars.

The Bay Area Rapid Transit, called BART, carries people

The photograph above shows a BART train. BART carries commuters between the suburbs and San Francisco. You can see the skyline of the city in the background of the picture. The photograph at the bottom of page 115 shows a cable car on Hyde Street in San Francisco. The city is located on San Francisco Bay.

between San Francisco and the suburbs. BART uses electric trains. In the city, the trains run underground. Outside the city, the trains run above the ground.

Many people like to ride BART. During rush hours, trains enter and leave the city every few minutes. This helps people get to work or to their homes quickly.

Once in the city, people may use taxis, buses, and **cable cars.** Cable cars run on rails and are pulled by a steel cable moving under the street. These cars are a safe way to travel up and down the steep hills of San Francisco. Cable cars are a special kind of transportation in this beautiful city.

CHECKUP

1. What is a commuter?
2. Why is it important to use oil wisely?
3. How are people trying to use less gasoline?
4. Name some ways that people living near San Francisco can travel to work in the city.

KEY FACTS

1. Natural resources often shape the growth and development of a city or town.

2. Small towns have fewer people and buildings than cities have.

3. Suburbs are communities located near large cities.

4. Many people who live in suburbs commute to their jobs in the nearby city.

5. Commuters use a variety of transportation, including automobiles, buses, and trains.

6. A car pool is a good example of how people can use less gasoline.

VOCABULARY QUIZ

Write the numbers 1 to 10 on a sheet of paper. Match the words with their meanings below.

a. sawmill   f. rush hour
b. commuter   g. suburb
c. barbecue   h. blacksmith
d. car pool   i. cable car
e. trail ride   j. traffic

1. The time of day when most people are going to work or coming home

2. A building where machines cut tree trunks into boards

3. A group of people who ride together in an automobile and take turns driving their cars

4. A kind of transportation used by people in San Francisco

5. Cars, trucks, buses, and people moving along a street or highway

6. A gathering of people at which meat is roasted over an open fire

7. A trip on horseback along a planned route

8. Person who puts shoes on horses

9. Person who travels regularly between suburb and city

10. A community near a city

REVIEW QUESTIONS

1. How would you define a volunteer fire department?

2. What are some problems caused by people driving to work?

3. Besides the automobile, name some other ways that people can travel to work.

4. How is living in a small town different from living in a large city?

ACTIVITIES

1. Pretend you are going on a trail ride. You have only two saddlebags. What would you pack for one week?

2. If you were old enough to drive to school, with whom could you car pool? Draw a map to show how your car pool would go from your home to school.

READING A MAP

SKILLS PRACTICE

Every community is made up of neighborhoods. Look at the map of a neighborhood below. Answer the questions on a sheet of paper.

1. What kinds of buildings are in this neighborhood?

2. On what streets are the stores?

3. If you live on the corner of Church Street and Miller Street, in which directions would you walk to school?

4. Using the scale, how far is it from the Library to the Firehouse?

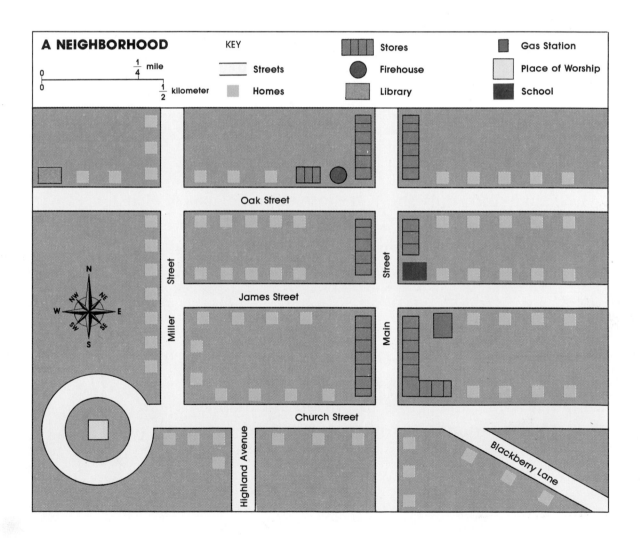

A NEIGHBORHOOD

KEY — Streets, Homes, Stores, Firehouse, Library, Gas Station, Place of Worship, School

Oak Street, James Street, Church Street, Miller Street, Main Street, Highland Avenue, Blackberry Lane

2/UNIT REVIEW

1. Many communities began and grew because they were located near natural resources.—*How did natural resources help each of the following communities grow? (a) Cincinnati, Ohio (b) Denver, Colorado (c) Miami Beach, Florida (d) Humble, Texas.*

2. A few communities, such as Washington, D.C., began as planned communities. — *Why is Washington called a government city?*

3. People live in large cities, small towns, and suburbs. — *If you could choose the kind of community you wanted to live in, which would it be? For what reasons would you choose that kind of community?*

4. In each community there are places for people to work. —*What kinds of work do people in your community do? Make a list.*

5. In each community there are interesting places to visit and fun things to do. — *If a friend from another state was to visit you, what special places in and near your community would you show your friend? Why would you visit those places?*

6. People who live and work in different communities need transportation. — *If you were a factory owner, what forms of transportation would you need? Why? If you were a commuter, what forms of transportation would you need? Why? What do you think would happen to a community if its transportation system stopped working?*

Farms and Resources Support Our Communities

Farms Long Ago and Now

VOCABULARY

| crops | fertilizer |
| income | harvest |

How farming has changed
Long ago most of the people in our country lived on small farms. They worked hard and did almost everything for themselves. They made most of their clothing. They made most of their tools and the things they used in their houses.

Farmers also grew their own food. They planted vegetables and fruits. They raised cows, chickens, and pigs. Most of the time they were able to grow only enough food to feed their own family. Once in a while, farmers had more food than they needed for themselves. Then they would sell the extra food. They used the money they got to buy some of the things they could not make.

Over the years, farming has changed. Today farmers are able to grow plants in large amounts for food and other uses. They sell these **crops** to earn money, or **income**. Then they use part of their income to buy different goods they need.

People living on farms no longer make most of their clothing, tools, and household goods. Instead, they buy most of these things in stores. Many farmers now buy most of the food they eat from supermarkets or grocery stores. They buy what they do not grow on their own farms.

Many years ago, most people lived on farms. Not as many people live on farms today. Most Americans live in towns or cities. Even though there are fewer farms in the United States, these farms produce more food than ever before.

The cornfields of Nebraska stretch for miles. Nebraska is one of the leading farming states in the United States. Find Nebraska on the map on pages 16–17.

Modern ways of farming

There are several reasons why farms produce more food today. One reason is the use of **fertilizer.** Farmers put fertilizer in the soil to make the crops grow bigger and stronger. They also use new kinds of seeds. Healthier plants grow from these seeds.

Another reason why farms produce more food is because of modern farm machines. It once took days for farmers to plow the land. Horses pulled the plow. Then farmers planted seeds by hand. Later in the year farmers spent time taking care of the growing plants and **harvesting,** or gathering in, the crops. Much of the farm work was done by hand.

Farmers could only take care of small farms.

Today most farmers use large machines to plow, plant, and harvest much faster. This means they can farm more land because they are able to take care of more land. Farms are much larger than they once were.

In the rest of the chapter you will learn about some different kinds of farms. These farms supply food for our communities.

CHECKUP

1. Describe how farms of today are different from farms of long ago.
2. Where do most people in the United States live today? Where did most people live many years ago?

This large machine is used to harvest grapes.

A Dairy Farm

Milk and butter for your table

In different parts of the United States, farmers raise many different crops and animals. In states such as Wisconsin, California, New York, Pennsylvania, and Minnesota, many farmers have **dairy farms.**

What is a dairy farm? It is a farm on which the main work is raising milk cows. Some milk is made into products such as butter, cheese, and ice cream. Of course, some of the milk is used for drinking milk, too. These products are all called dairy products.

One of the most important dairy states is Wisconsin. Here almost 2 million dairy cows graze in the **pastures.** Wisconsin is the leading milk-producing state. It also produces a great deal of the country's cheese and butter. For this reason, Wisconsin is sometimes called America's Dairyland. Turn to the map on pages 208–209 and find the state of Wisconsin. Then find the other

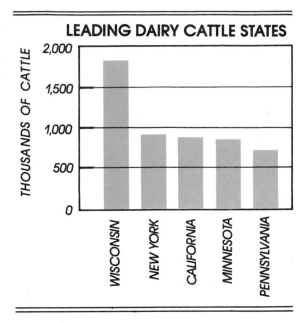

LEADING DAIRY CATTLE STATES

About how many dairy cattle does New York have?

important dairy states named in the bar graph above.

Now that you know what a dairy farm is, you can find out what it is like to live on one.

A visit with Annie   "Hi, my name is Annie. I live in Wisconsin. My mom and dad own a dairy farm. We have about 500 cows.

"Most of our cows are called Holsteins (hōl′ stīns). They have black-and-white coats. Holsteins produce the most milk. One of

123

These black-and-white cows are called Holsteins. They produce more milk than any other breed of dairy cattle.

"My dad tells me that dairy farms have really changed since he was a boy. He used to milk the cows by hand. Dairy farms needed many helpers then.

"Today our cows are milked by machine. We take the cows to our milking room. The room is very clean. My job is to help wash and brush the cows before they are milked. We milk the

The milking room at a modern dairy farm is kept very clean.

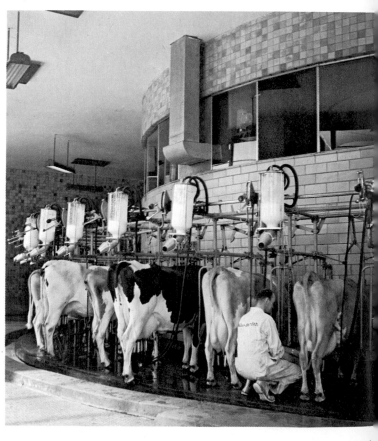

our Holsteins—we call her Molly—produces about 55 quarts (52 L) of milk a day.

"Some of our cows are Jerseys. They are a different breed, or kind, of cow from the Holsteins. Jersey cows produce less milk, but their milk has more natural fat in it. The fat, called butterfat, is used to make butter.

cows early in the morning and late in the afternoon, so I have to work twice a day. This means I am up every morning before the sun comes up.

"As the cows are milked, the milk passes through pipes to the milk house. Here it is cooled. The milk is kept here until it is put into a tank truck. The truck takes the milk to a **creamery.** At the

This is a cheese market in the Netherlands.

There are hundreds of cheeses. Here workers are making Roquefort (rōk' fərt) cheese.

creamery, the milk is made into butter and other dairy products.

"In the summer the cows go out to the fields during the day. They graze on the grass in the pastures. In the winter we keep them in a barn. This protects them from the weather. We feed the cows **hay** in the winter. Hay is grass that is cut and dried. It is often used as food for cows.

"Our cows are always eating. Mom says that each cow eats about 40 to 60 pounds (18 to 27 kg) of food a day. Each one also drinks about 8 gallons (30 L) of water a day."

CHECKUP
1. Name some dairy products.
2. Name five leading dairy states.
3. What is a creamery?

125

A Vegetable Farm

─VOCABULARY─
greenhouse   irrigation

Fresh vegetables for your table   Vegetables are the parts of plants that people eat. Corn, potatoes, lettuce, and peas are all vegetables. Can you name some others?

Vegetables are important foods. They give us vitamins and minerals. These are special substances that the body needs in small amounts. People need vitamins and minerals for growth and good health. Eating many different vegetables is a good way to get enough vitamins and minerals.

Some vegetable farms are located far from cities. These farms are usually large and cover many acres. Often only one or two kinds of vegetables are grown on them.

Some of the largest vegetable farms are in southern California, southern Florida, Arizona, and Texas. These places have a warm climate all year, so farmers can grow vegetables year round.

Besides a warm climate, vegetables need water to grow. Many farmers use a special way, or method, of watering called **irrigation.** They use ditches, canals, or pipes to carry water to lands that are dry. In southern California, for example, there is almost no rain in the summer. The farmlands become very dry, so farmers irrigate the soil. That way they do not have to depend as much on rainfall.

After the vegetables have been harvested, farmers send them to

It is harvest time in this California onion field.

Irrigation means farmers do not have to depend as much on rainfall. A farmer who irrigates can bring just the right amount of water to the land when it is needed.

A visit with Tommy "My family owns a vegetable farm in New York. It is near New York City. Our farm is small. We have only a few acres of land, but we grow many different kinds of vegetables. We grow most of them outside during the summer months.

"During the winter months, we raise a few vegetables in our **greenhouse.** The greenhouse is a large building. It has windows in the roof. This lets in the light that the plants need to grow.

"The greenhouse is heated in the winter and cooled in the

markets all over the United States. The vegetables travel many miles by trains, trucks, and airplanes. People in the northern states can buy fresh vegetables even when there is snow on the ground in their town or city.

Tommy will tell you about another kind of vegetable farm. As you read, think of the ways in which Tommy's farm is different from the farms you have just learned about.

Cucumbers are growing in this large greenhouse in Tucson, Arizona. Tucson is located at 32° north latitude and 111° west longitude.

This farm stand has tomatoes and watermelons for sale.

summer. We can grow vegetables all year round in the greenhouse. Even when there is snow on the ground, the plants in the greenhouse are warm. We grow mostly tomatoes in our greenhouse. We have fresh tomatoes all year long.

"Trucks carry almost all of our vegetables to stores in New York City. Every summer, though, my sister and I set up a vegetable stand. We put some tables by the road that goes past our farm. We have some signs that tell what we are selling. Many people stop. They like our vegetables because they are fresh. Every morning I pick what we are going to sell that day."

CHECKUP

1. Why are vitamins and minerals important?
2. How is Tommy's vegetable farm different from a large vegetable farm in Texas?

128

A Wheat Farm

—VOCABULARY—

| combine | grain elevator |

"For amber waves of grain"
These words are from the song "America, the Beautiful." They describe the huge fields of wheat stretching across the land. When the wind blows, the yellow-brown stalks of wheat sway back and forth in the breeze. They look like a golden ocean.

Wheat is one of the world's most important food crops. It is grown in many places throughout the world. In the United States most of the wheat is grown in five states. The graph on page 221 shows the leading wheat-producing states. These states are part of an area called the Great Plains. Find the Great Plains on the map on page 16.

Now that you know where wheat is grown in our country, you can find out more about a wheat farm.

A visit with Karen "My name is Karen. I live on a farm in Kansas. We grow wheat on our farm. You may have eaten some things made from our wheat. Most of our wheat is used to make flour. People make bread, rolls, cookies, and cakes from flour. Some of our wheat is used to make breakfast cereals.

To harvest the wheat, farmers use a machine called a combine.

After the harvest, wheat is stored in tall grain elevators.

"We grow winter wheat. It is planted in the fall. It stops growing in the winter when it is covered with snow. In the spring it starts growing again. When it is first planted, the wheat looks like grass. Later it grows to about 5 feet (2 m) and turns a beautiful golden color.

"Mom and Dad can tell when the wheat is ready for harvesting or cutting. They break the top, or head, off the wheat. Then they chew it. They say that the way the wheat breaks up tells them if it is ready for harvesting.

"We use a large machine to help harvest the wheat. This machine is called a **combine.** It does the job that three other machines once did. It cuts the wheat. It separates the grain from the stem and leaves of the plant. It also cleans the grain.

"Trucks take the wheat to nearby **grain elevators.** In these tall buildings the wheat is stored until it is sent to flour mills. The wheat travels to the mills in special train cars. At the mills the wheat is ground into flour."

CHECKUP
1. Name the leading wheat-producing states.
2. What are some products made from wheat?
3. How is the wheat harvested?
4. What is the purpose of a grain elevator?

130

A Citrus Farm

Have you had your vitamin C today? In this chapter you have learned about several different kinds of farms. Now take a look at still another kind of farm—a citrus farm.

In the United States, there are more **citrus fruits** grown than any other fruit. Citrus fruits grow on trees. Some citrus fruits you may recognize are oranges, lemons, limes, and grapefruits.

Many people like oranges. They drink the sweet juice or peel the skin and eat the orange sections. Oranges are rich in vitamin C.

You will almost always find oranges in grocery stores. Carlos will tell you how they get there.

A visit with Carlos "My name is Carlos. My family owns a citrus farm in Florida. We grow oranges.

"The orange trees grow well here because we have a warm climate. Every once in a while, the weather turns cold. Then we

Like all citrus fruits, oranges grow on trees in warm climates.

Heaters in the orange grove protect the fruit from freezing temperatures.

At the packing house, workers sort the oranges according to size and quality.

worry. If it gets cold enough to freeze water, then it is cold enough to freeze our oranges and our trees. This would hurt our orange crop. When we think our trees might freeze, we turn on some heaters in the fields. These heaters warm the air and help protect the trees and fruit from the cold.

"The trees are about 30 feet (9 m) tall. In the spring, they are covered with white flowers. A part of each flower becomes an orange. When the oranges are ready for picking, workers use ladders to climb into the trees. The workers carefully pull the oranges off the trees. They do not want to bruise the fruit. During the harvest season my father hires many orange pickers.

"We take the fruit to the packing house. Here the oranges are washed. Then they are sized. This means they are placed in boxes with other oranges that are the same size.

"From the packing house most of our oranges go to a **cannery.** This is a factory that cans and freezes orange juice. The rest of our oranges are sold to stores and some may end up in your grocery store."

CHECKUP
1. Name the most familiar citrus fruits.
2. How do citrus farmers protect the orange trees from freezing?
3. What is a cannery?

Ranching

What is a ranch? You can probably answer that question. You have seen **ranches** or parts of ranches. You may have seen a ranch on a television show or in a movie. You may have passed by a ranch when you were traveling. Some of you may even live on a ranch.

The dictionary tells us that a ranch is a large farm for raising cattle, sheep, or horses. These animals are called **livestock.** Livestock need a lot of grass to eat. This means that a ranch has to have many acres of grassland to feed the animals. Some ranch lands are very dry. Little grass can grow there. Places such as this may need 50 acres (20 ha) of land to feed one cow.

Beef cattle are raised for their meat. We eat the meat of cattle as roast beef, hamburger, and beef hot dogs. Texas produces the most beef cattle. Other leading beef cattle states are Iowa, Nebraska, Kansas, and Oklahoma.

One of the largest ranches in the country is the Parker Ranch. It is on the island of Hawaii. Find the Hawaiian Islands on the map on pages 208—209. You can see that Hawaii is the largest island. It is about 2,400 miles (3,900 km) from the rest of the United States.

The Parker Ranch has more Hereford (her′ fərd) cattle than any ranch in the world. Herefords are white-faced cattle. The ranch itself has about 330,000 acres (134,000 ha) of land.

This is a sheep ranch in New Zealand. Find New Zealand on the map on page 216.

133

Life on a cattle ranch There are cattle ranches in different parts of the United States. For the cattle most days are the same. They usually eat early in the morning. In the middle of the day the cattle rest under trees. In the afternoon they go to the watering hole for water. Then they eat again until dark.

Ranchers have busy days. They have to fix broken fences. They also check the watering hole to be sure there is enough water for the animals. They put out blocks of salt for the cattle to lick. The animals need salt in their diet.

Ranchers also plant and care for crops of hay. Hay is used as food for the livestock. When snow covers the ground the cattle cannot find food on their own. Then ranchers spread hay on the ground for them to eat.

A cowhand herds cattle on a ranch in New Mexico.

A rancher mends a broken fence in the pasture. Fences are important because they keep the cattle from straying away from the ranch.

A cowhand on a Montana ranch feeds hay to the cattle during a snowstorm.

Ranchers take special care of their livestock in other ways, too. Sometimes a calf, or baby cow, becomes sick. When this happens ranchers move the calf and its mother from the fields to the barn. Here they can give the sick calf special care.

A horse is still a cowhand's best friend. Today, however, newer ways of transportation are being used on ranches. Ranchers use cars, trucks, and jeeps. Some ranchers may use snowmobiles, motorcycles, and helicopters.

After a snowstorm in Wyoming, a rancher uses a snowmobile to herd cattle. It is much easier for the rancher to travel by machine than to ride a horse in the deep snow.

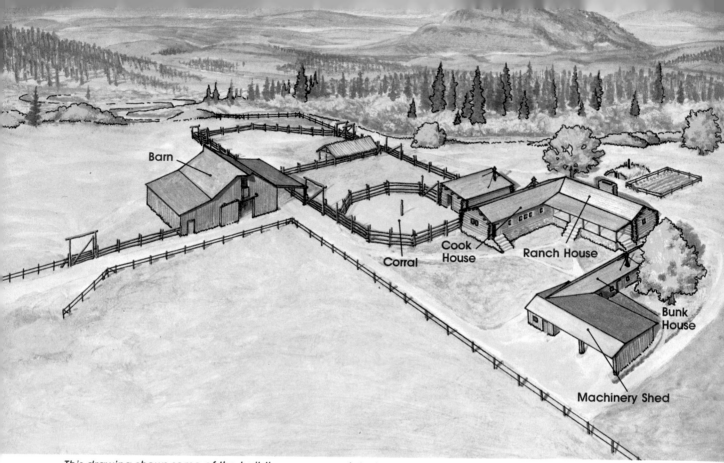

Barn

Corral

Cook House

Ranch House

Bunk House

Machinery Shed

This drawing shows some of the buildings on a ranch today.

The drawing above shows what a ranch might look like today. Find the ranch house. This is where the owner of the ranch lives. A large barn is usually close by. Some of the cattle and horses are kept there. Hay is also kept in the barn. Often there will be a building to keep the trucks, tractors, trailers, and tools used on the ranch.

Another part of the ranch is the **corral.** This fenced area is usually close to the ranch house.

Horses and cattle are put in the corral when they are first brought to the ranch or before they are taken to be sold.

Today many ranchers use radios. The radios help them talk to the cowhands in their jeeps or trucks.

CHECKUP

1. Why do ranches need to have a lot of land?
2. Describe some of the things a rancher does.
3. Besides riding a horse, in what other ways might a rancher travel around the ranch?

136

A Livestock Show and Rodeo

What is a livestock show?
Ranchers are always trying to raise better animals. Livestock shows help them. At the shows, ranchers see the prize-winning animals and talk with their owners. They compare ways of feeding their livestock. Ranchers may go to classes that teach new ways to care for animals. They can also buy and sell animals.

You can see all kinds of animals at the show.

At a livestock show, prizes are given to the finest animals.

the show. These animals are looked at carefully by judges. The judges give first-place, second-place, and third-place ribbons to the best animals.

Many of the animals are sold during the livestock show. **Auctions** are held each day. At an auction the animals are sold to the people who will pay the highest price.

This is a cattle auction. The animal in the ring will be sold to the person who pays the highest price for it.

One of the biggest livestock shows is held every year in Houston, Texas. People from all over the world bring their animals to this livestock show.

Some high school students raise animals and enter them in

What is a rodeo? The Houston Rodeo takes place at the same time as the Livestock Show. A **rodeo** is a series of contests that shows the skills of cowgirls and cowboys. *Rodeo* is from a Spanish word that has become part of our language. In English it means "to surround" or "to round up." Rodeos are held in most parts of the United States. The Houston Rodeo is one of the largest.

Each rodeo has many different events. An event such as bull riding tests a cowhand against an animal. The person must stay on the animal for a certain number of seconds.

Other rodeo events test a person against a clock. One such event is steer wrestling. The cowhand jumps from the horse onto a running steer. Then the cowhand grabs the horns of the steer and tries to wrestle the animal to the ground. The person who wins this event is the one who brings the steer down in the least amount of time. Other timed events include steer roping and barrel racing.

The Houston Rodeo is held in the Astrodome. The Astrodome is a big covered stadium. It holds more than 50,000 people. Baseball, football, and other sports are played here, too.

CHECKUP

1. How does a livestock show help ranchers to raise better animals?
2. What is an auction?
3. How would you define *rodeo?*
4. Describe some of the different events you might see at a rodeo.

In the bull-riding event, the rider hangs on tightly with one hand.

5 / CHAPTER REVIEW

KEY FACTS

1. Today many more Americans live in cities than live on farms and ranches.
2. Many American farmers use modern farming methods and the newest farm machines to help them grow more food.
3. Farms and ranches produce many different crops and animals, such as vegetables, citrus fruits, wheat, and beef and dairy cattle.

VOCABULARY QUIZ

Copy the sentences below and fill in the blanks with the right vocabulary term. Write on a sheet of paper.

a. auction
b. creamery
c. greenhouse
d. dairy farm
e. wheat
f. rodeo
g. livestock
h. hay
i. citrus fruits
j. income

1. Holstein and Jersey cows are found on a ____.
2. My friend was in the barrel race at the ____.
3. The combine helps farmers harvest their fields of ____.
4. Lemons and oranges are examples of ____.
5. The ____ keeps plants warm in the winter months.
6. Milk leaves the dairy and goes to the ____ where it is made into butter and other dairy products.
7. Sheep are sold at the ____ to buyers who will pay the highest price.
8. Farmers and ranchers buy many things with the ____ from their crops and animals.
9. Ranchers feed ____ to livestock.
10. Cattle, horses, and sheep are called ____.

REVIEW QUESTIONS

1. What are some changes that have taken place on farms and ranches over the years?
2. How are greenhouses used?
3. What are some dairy products? What are some wheat products?
4. Why is irrigation important?
5. Describe what takes place at a livestock show and rodeo.

ACTIVITIES

1. Find out what farm products are grown in your state. If possible, bring one of these products to show in class.
2. Make a booklet of pictures showing farm products. Write the name of each product under the picture.

READING PICTOGRAPHS

SKILLS PRACTICE

The first pictograph below shows the number of people living on farms in four different years. The second graph shows the average size of farms in the same four years. Use the graphs to answer the following questions below.

1. What does each 🧍 stand for?
2. About how many people were living on farms in the United States (a) in 1950? (b) in 1960? (c) in 1970? (d) in 1980?
3. In 1980 were there more people or fewer people living on farms than there were in 1950?
4. What does each 🏠 stand for?
5. About how many acres did the average farm have (a) in 1950? (b) in 1960? (c) in 1970? (d) in 1980?
6. From 1950 to 1980 did farms become larger or smaller in size?

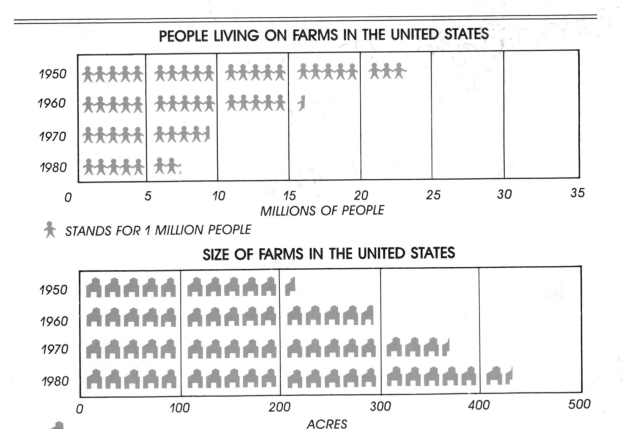

PEOPLE LIVING ON FARMS IN THE UNITED STATES

🧍 STANDS FOR 1 MILLION PEOPLE

SIZE OF FARMS IN THE UNITED STATES

🏠 STANDS FOR 20 ACRES

A Coal-Mining Community

```
┌─ VOCABULARY ──────────────┐
│  mineral         electricity  │
│  coal            fuel          │
│  mining                        │
└──────────────────────────────┘
```

Gifts from the earth The United States is a large country. It has many different kinds of natural resources. There are forests and farmlands. There are lakes and rivers. There are fish and wildlife.

Still another kind of natural resource is **minerals**. A mineral is a substance found in the earth. **Coal**, iron, gold, and copper are all minerals. Some minerals are near the surface of the earth. Other minerals are buried deep in the ground. Minerals are taken from the earth by digging them out. This is called **mining.**

In Chapter 3 you have read that cities began for many reasons. Some cities began and grew because they had some important natural resources. Every community does not have the same resources. Some have plenty of water. Others have good soil. Still others have minerals deep in the ground. What natural resources have helped your community develop?

In this chapter you will learn about several communities. Each has important natural resources. The first community you will read about has large deposits of coal.

What is coal? Coal is a valuable mineral. It is a black rock that will burn. When it is burned, coal makes energy in the form of heat. Some people use the heat from coal to warm their home and place of business.

The heat from burning coal can also run large motors that

The United States has about 215,000 coal miners. A miner produces an average of about 15 short tons (14 metric tons) of coal each day.

make **electricity**. Electricity is a form of energy that gives light and heat. People use electricity every day when they turn on electric lights.

Coal is one of the world's most important **fuels**. A fuel is anything that is burned to make heat or to make power for running machines. Coal is found on every continent. It is also found in 25 of the 50 states in the United States. The map on page 145 shows the location of coalfields in the United States. Does your state have deposits of coal?

Leading producers of coal
Turn now to page 220 and look at the two bar graphs about coal production. One graph shows world coal production. Which nation is the leading coal-producing country in the world? How much coal does it produce?

The second bar graph shows coal production in the United States. Which are the five leading states? Which state produces the most coal?

You can see from the graph that Pennsylvania is the third largest coal-producing state. Now

Miners used to dig the coal with picks and shovels. Today miners use different machines for digging, loading, and moving coal.

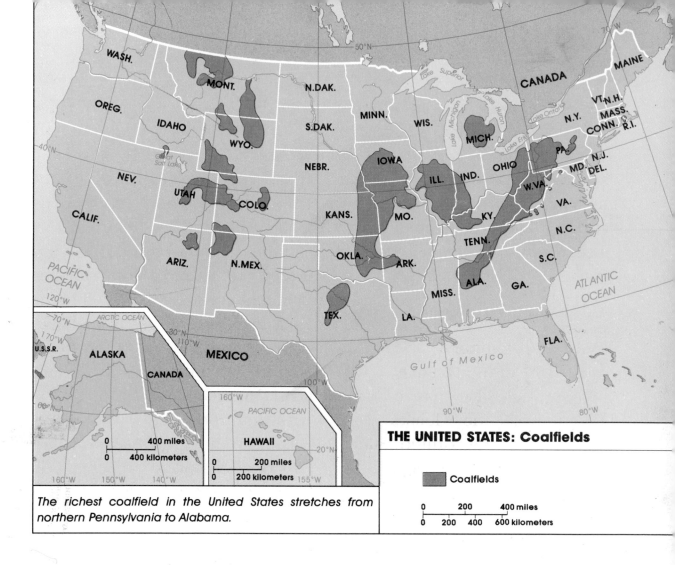

THE UNITED STATES: Coalfields

Coalfields

0   200   400 miles
0 200 400 600 kilometers

The richest coalfield in the United States stretches from northern Pennsylvania to Alabama.

find Pennsylvania on the map on this page. The map shows that there is a lot of coal mined in that state.

Working in the coal mines

There are a number of coal-mining towns in Pennsylvania. One such place is Scranton, a community in the northeastern part of the state. Scranton is located in a valley bordered by mountains.

It grew because there was coal in the area. Today many products are made in Scranton, but it is still known as a coal-mining community. Find Scranton on the map on pages 208–209.

Some of the people of Scranton work in coal mines or for mining companies. The coal is located deep under the ground, so the mines go down deep into the earth. The miners travel down the mine shaft on an elevator. The elevator is called a cage.

All the miners wear special shoes and caps, or helmets. The helmets and shoes are hard and strong. They protect a miner from getting hurt by falling pieces of rock or coal.

How is the coal taken out of a mine deep inside the earth?

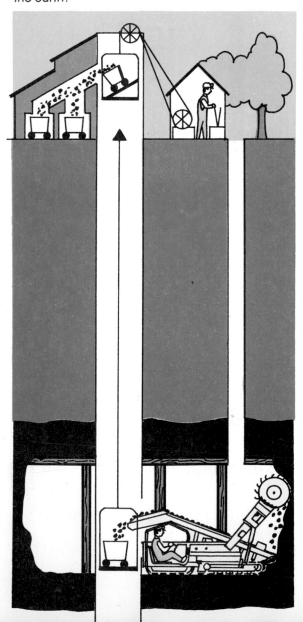

In the past, coal miners used picks and shovels to dig out the coal. Today machines do most of the work in coal mines. Miners must know how to run the different kinds of machines.

One machine digs out the coal and loads it onto a conveyor belt. The conveyor belt takes the coal to the mine train. The train carries the coal to the shaft. At the shaft, the coal is placed in an elevator and lifted to the surface. The drawing shows how the coal is taken up the mine shaft.

Once the coal reaches the surface of the ground, it is cleaned. This means the coal is first sorted into different sizes. Then it is washed and dried. Finally the coal is loaded onto trains, trucks, or barges. Much of the coal goes to electric power companies. They burn the coal to produce heat for running the machines that make electricity.

CHECKUP

1. What is a mineral?
2. Why is coal a valuable mineral?
3. Name some things miners wear that help to keep them safe in the mine.

An Oil-Drilling Community

Black gold   Every time you ride in a car, you are using **petroleum** (pə trō′ lē əm) and products made from petroleum. Petroleum is usually called oil. Gasoline is made from petroleum. The motor of each car needs oil in it. The oil helps the motor run better. Oil is used in making the rubber that goes into tires. The seats in your car may be made from oil products. If you drive on an asphalt (as′ fôlt) road, it, too, is made from petroleum products. People use oil or products made from oil every day.

Oil is a dark liquid that is found in the earth. Its many different uses make oil very valuable. This is why oil is sometimes called black gold.

Petroleum, like coal, is a fuel. Petroleum is also a nonrenewable (non ri nü′ ə bəl) resource. This means that once the oil is used, it cannot be replaced. The earth

Petroleum is taken from the ground by drilling wells. Oil drillers operate the equipment.

has only a certain amount of oil. After it is used, there will not be any more. Oil is not like some other resources, such as soil or plants. We cannot make or grow more oil.

Leading oil producers   Like coal, oil is found deep in the ground. Look at the map on page

149. It shows where oil is located in the United States. Which states have large oil fields?

Turn now to page 220 and look at the two bar graphs about oil production. One graph shows oil production in the United States. Which are the five leading states?

The other bar graph shows world oil production. Which nation produces the most oil? What are the other four leading oil-producing nations? Find each of these countries on the map on pages 206–207.

A derrick is a steel tower that holds the drilling equipment.

Drilling for oil Oil is taken from the ground by drilling wells. An oil **derrick** holds the drilling equipment. A derrick is a steel tower. It is usually between 80 and 200 feet (24 to 61 m) high.

A drill **bit** is placed on the end of a piece of pipe. This bit will cut and break up rocks as it drills deep into the earth. The pipe and the bit are turned by a large motor. As the bit drills deeper, more pipe is added. Some oil wells go down many feet. In Oklahoma, one well was dug almost six miles deep.

An offshore oil platform Rich deposits of oil have been found off the shores of some countries. To reach the offshore oil, workers drill wells in the ocean floor. They work from an **offshore oil platform**. It has a derrick and drilling machinery. It also has living space for the workers. A platform is sometimes miles from any land. The offshore wells are often drilled in very deep water.

We are going to visit an offshore platform, often called a

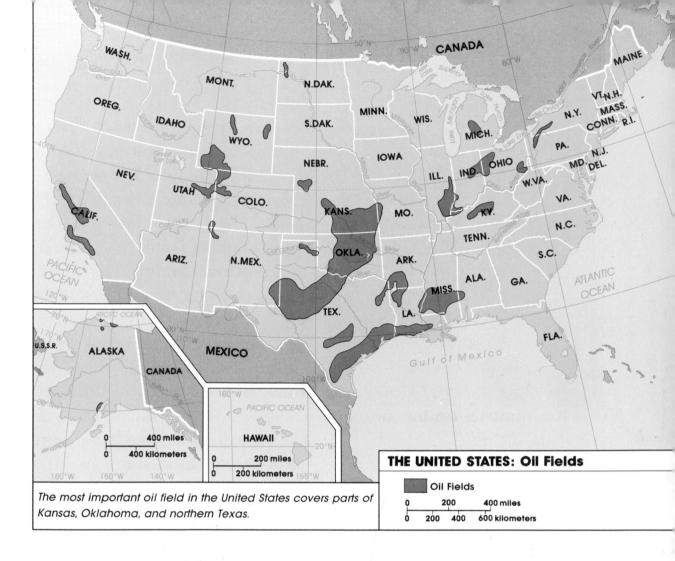

THE UNITED STATES: Oil Fields

Oil Fields

| 0 | 200 | 400 miles |
| 0 | 200 | 400 | 600 kilometers |

The most important oil field in the United States covers parts of Kansas, Oklahoma, and northern Texas.

rig. Our guide is a man who takes workers and supplies to these rigs. We will meet him in Morgan City, Louisiana. Morgan City is a small town about 45 miles (72 km) south of Baton Rouge. It is only about 15 miles (24 km) from the Gulf of Mexico. Find Morgan City on the map on page 209.

"My name is Mike Mayeaux (mī yü'). It is my job to take workers from Morgan City to many of the rigs in the Gulf. My company uses boats and helicopters to do this. Most heavy supplies and many of the workers go to the rigs on the boats. But I fly one of our helicopters.

"I fly to several rigs every day. Because it is so hard to get to these rigs, the workers will stay on them for a week or two at a time. I spend most of my time taking new groups of workers to the rigs.

On this offshore oil platform, you can see the derrick and the buildings where the workers live.

"The rig that we are flying to is about 30 miles (48 km) from here. As we go, we will see several other rigs. One of these is a rig that is being taken into the Gulf. The rig is pulled by two tug boats. When the boats get to the right place, the rig will be let down slowly. Its legs will stand on the floor of the Gulf.

"We will land our helicopter on the flat part of the rig. From the air, the rig looks small.

"Now that we are on the rig, we can see how big it is. The derrick over there stands 80 feet (24 m) tall. That is where the drilling takes place. The building next to the derrick has motors in it. These motors turn the pipe and the drill.

"The large building to our left is where the workers live while they are out here. There are 45 workers here all of the time. They eat and sleep in that building. There is also a room where they can watch TV or play games.

"The only time that the drilling stops here is when there is a **hurricane**. This is a storm with high winds and heavy rain. When a hurricane comes close to a rig, the waves in the water might be over 20 feet (6 m) high. The boats cannot reach the rig, so I have to fly out and help get the workers off.

"I have been flying to the rigs for three years. During that time, I have seen this rig in three different places. In the last two places, they did not find any oil. I hope that this time they will finally find oil."

CHECKUP

1. What is a derrick?
2. What does the drill bit do?
3. Why are offshore oil platforms used?
4. How are workers and supplies taken to the offshore oil platforms?

Oil from the Ground to You

Refining the oil   What do you think happens to oil once it is taken out of the ground? It goes to a **refinery**. At a refinery, machines make the oil pure. Then the oil is changed into different products that people can use. There are oil refineries all over the world.

Moving the oil   Oil has to be moved from the oil well to the refinery. Oil and oil products also have to be moved from the refineries to your community. Railroad tank cars, trucks, and ships called tankers are all used to transport petroleum.

Another way of moving oil is through **pipelines**. A pipeline is made by welding many pipes together. Some pipelines are more than 3,000 miles (4,827 km) long. Usually a pipeline is placed about 3 feet (1 m) under the ground. Sometimes a pipeline is built above the ground. Pumps

More than half of the Trans-Alaska Pipeline is built above the ground on supports.

A refinery is a huge factory where oil is changed into different products.

push the petroleum through the pipeline.

One pipeline crosses Alaska, our largest state. It was one of the most difficult pipelines to build. It crosses rivers, streams, and mountains. The Trans-Alaska Pipeline stretches for 800 miles (1,300 km).

Oil from other countries The United States uses more petroleum than any other nation. We do not produce all the oil we need, so we buy oil from other countries. Much of the oil we buy comes from Saudi Arabia (soud′ ē ə rā′ bē ə). Find Saudi Arabia on the world map on pages 206–207.

Saudi Arabian oil is pumped from the wells and sent through pipelines to port cities. At the ports the oil is placed in large storage tanks. The oil is held in these tanks until it is sent through other pipelines to the tankers. These huge ships carry millions of gallons of oil to the United States. The tankers also carry Saudi Arabian oil to other nations in the world.

This is a 121,000-ton tanker named the Arco Fairbanks. *It is shown near the port of Valdez in southern Alaska.*

CHECKUP

1. What happens at an oil refinery?
2. How is oil moved through a pipeline?
3. Name the pipeline that crosses Alaska.
4. Why does the United States buy oil from other countries?

Fishing Communities

Good harbors   Oceans, lakes, and rivers are valuable resources. From them we get many different kinds of seafood. People all over the world eat seafood.

Many communities began as fishing communities. They usually have good harbors. A harbor is a protected body of water. It helps keep the fishing boats safe from storms.

Fishing is still important in many communities along the coasts. Many people earn their living by fishing. Each morning they go out in boats to the fishing grounds. Each night they come back into the harbor with the catches of fish. If it was a good day, there will be plenty of fish to sell.

Some fishing boats travel far out into the ocean. They go where the ocean water is very deep. These boats are very large. They can stay out at sea for weeks. They use big nets to catch many different kinds of fish.

This aerial photograph shows many small boats in a protected harbor in Maine.

Many people earn their living by fishing. Many other people like to eat seafood.

Lobsters are caught in wooden traps called pots.

Lobsters from Maine One kind of fishing is **lobster** fishing. Many people like to eat lobster meat.

Have you ever been in a grocery store or fish market and seen a glass tank filled with water and some sea animals? The animals are dark green or dark blue in color. They have a hard shell and two big claws. They are called lobsters. They may have been caught in the ocean along the coast of Maine. Find Maine on the map on pages 208–209.

Lobsters are caught in traps called pots. A trap is made of wood. Pieces of fish are put in the trap. The trap has a rope tied to it. The trap is put into the water. Rocks are put into the trap to make it sink to the bottom of the ocean. The other end of the rope is tied to a small block of painted wood. The wood floats. This float, as it is called, shows where the lobster pot is placed. The lobster goes into the trap to eat the fish. Once inside, the lobster cannot get out.

The lobster pot is pulled out of the water almost every day. If there is a lobster in the pot, it is taken out and put in a tank of water. More pieces of fish are put into the trap and it is dropped back into the water.

CHECKUP

1. Why is a good harbor important to a fishing community?
2. How are lobsters caught?

Conserving Our Natural Resources

The need for conservation
The earth is full of natural resources that we use every day. However, we have to be careful how we use these valuable resources.

If we cut down too many trees, the forests will disappear. Then there will be no trees to use to build houses or to make paper. There will be no place for wild animals and wild birds to live and hide. People will not be able to camp in the forests.

If we dump trash and garbage into the rivers and oceans, the waters will become **polluted**, or dirty. The dirty water will be unhealthy for people to use. It will also be harmful to the fish and other water animals.

If we let factories pour smoke into the air, our air will become polluted. Polluted air can make our eyes sting and fill with tears. It can make paint on buildings fade and peel off. It can eat away metal. It can kill trees and hurt other plants. Polluted air hurts almost everything it touches.

Trees, water, and air are some of our most important natural resources. We need to take care of them so they will not be spoiled and wasted. This good use of natural resources is called **conservation.**

Waste from a steel mill had polluted this part of Lake Erie. Today the lake is much cleaner.

President Theodore Roosevelt
Conservation is not a new idea. Years ago President Theodore Roosevelt was interested in conservation. When he was young, he was a sick boy. He spent much of his time in the out-of-doors. He walked through forests full of wild flowers, plants, and tall trees. He watched birds and wild animals. He learned their names and saw how they lived. He learned that many animals need plants for food.

Life in the out-of-doors made Teddy Roosevelt's body stronger. It also taught him many things about nature. He learned to care for the land.

As President, Mr. Roosevelt wanted to protect America's natural resources. He talked to members of **Congress** about the need for conservation. Congress is the group of people who are picked to make **laws** for the United States. Laws are rules that people must obey.

In 1903 President Roosevelt visited the Yosemite Valley in California. Today the valley is part of Yosemite National Park.

Forest Service rangers plant new tree seedlings after a forest fire.

Together the President and Congress made millions of acres of beautiful forest lands into **national forests**. A national forest belongs to all the people. No one may buy this land.

Rangers take care of the national forests. These people work for the government. They decide which trees should be cut and which should be left standing. Rangers plant new trees. They also guard against forest fires. If a fire does start, they work quickly to put it out.

While Theodore Roosevelt was President, much land became national forests and national parks. Americans remember this President. He helped people understand how important it is to use our natural resources with care.

Conservation efforts Today many people are showing that they care about the earth. In cities such as Atlanta, Georgia, and Pittsburgh, Pennsylvania, people have worked together to make the air cleaner. People have worked hard to clean up the polluted waters of the Hudson River in New York, and Lake Erie. People have worked to get laws passed protecting certain kinds of wildlife.

Danger for the salmon One kind of wildlife that needs protection is salmon (sam′ ən). Salmon are one of our most important fishes. Every year millions of people eat salmon.

These fish are born in the freshwater streams of Oregon, Washington, and Alaska. After they are born, they swim to the Pacific Ocean to live. When the fish are ready to lay their eggs, they swim back up the rivers and streams to the fresh water where they were born. Here more salmon are born.

Years ago, Native Americans known as the Chinook lived along the Columbia River. The Columbia flows between Oregon

The Chinook and other Native Americans living in the northwestern United States found plenty of food in the forests, rivers, and ocean.

and Washington. Find this river and the two states on the map on pages 208–209. The Chinook ate salmon that they caught in the river. There were many salmon then.

Today, there are fewer salmon in the Columbia River. In the past 50 years, dams have been built. Dams, such as the Bonneville Dam, block the water of the Columbia. As the water is let through the dam, the water runs motors that make electricity. The electricity is used by the people of nearby cities, such as Portland, Oregon.

Salmon cannot swim through the dams, so special fish ladders have been built. These ladders help salmon swim upstream to the fresh water where they lay their eggs. The fish ladders help protect salmon.

A fish hatchery   Another way of protecting salmon is a **fish hatchery**. Thousands of salmon are born in hatcheries every year. The fish are raised at the hatchery until they are big enough to be put into the rivers and swim to the Pacific Ocean.

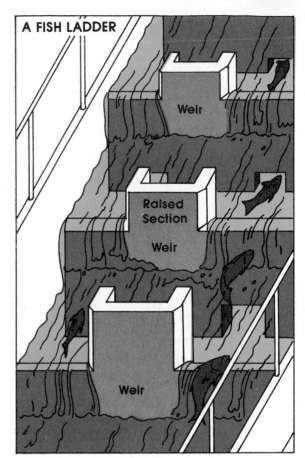

A FISH LADDER

Weir

Raised Section

Weir

Weir

Salmon move up the "steps" of the fish ladder by leaping from pool to pool. They may also swim through holes at the bottom of the weirs.

Fish hatcheries are one part of salmon conservation. Large numbers of fish are caught each year. Some salmon are killed by wastes that pollute the rivers. The purpose of fish hatcheries is to be sure there are always enough salmon.

CHECKUP

1. Why must people be careful about how they use the earth's natural resources?
2. Why was Theodore Roosevelt interested in conservation?
3. Describe a ranger's job.
4. What is a fish hatchery?

KEY FACTS

1. Coal is a valuable natural resource that is mined in many parts of the United States.

2. Petroleum is another valuable natural resource. People use oil and oil products every day.

3. Coal and oil are important fuels.

4. The oceans, lakes, and rivers supply fish, lobster, and other seafood.

5. Many people earn their living by fishing.

6. People must learn how to use and care for the earth's many natural resources.

VOCABULARY QUIZ

Copy the sentences below and fill in the blanks with the right vocabulary term. Write your answers on a separate sheet of paper.

a. coal   f. conservation
b. derrick   g. pollute
c. refinery   h. fuel
d. pipelines   i. lobsters
e. hatchery   j. petroleum

1. A ____ helps drill for oil.

2. People ____ the water when they throw garbage into it.

3. A rock that burns is ____.

4. Much of our oil is carried across the country through ____.

5. Young salmon are often raised at a fish ____.

6. A large ____ changes petroleum into products that people use.

7. Traps are placed in the ocean water to catch ____.

8. Tankers carry ____ from Saudi Arabia to the United States.

9. Taking care of natural resources so that they will not be spoiled or wasted is called ____.

10. Like coal, oil is a ____.

REVIEW QUESTIONS

1. How is coal mining today different from mining in the past?

2. Describe life on an offshore oil platform.

3. What is meant by a nonrenewable resource?

4. What is a lobster pot? What is the purpose of a lobster float?

5. Why is there a need to protect salmon? What dangers face salmon?

ACTIVITY

Choose one natural resource that has helped your community. Collect pictures of this resource. Place these pictures in a booklet. Then write a short report about that resource. Use the library to find information.

USING AN INDEX

MAIN IDEAS IN A BOOK

There are several parts to most books. Your social studies book has a table of contents, an atlas, and a glossary. Your book also has an index. An index lists the main things found in a book. Words in an index are arranged in alphabetical order.

Suppose you remember reading about oil, but you forget where. You can turn to the index and find the words beginning with *O*. Then you can look at the list until you find *Oil*. The numbers after the word *Oil* are the pages on which you would find facts about oil.

ENTRY WORDS AND SUBENTRIES

The main words in an index are called entry words. Sometimes there are other words listed just below the entry word. These words are called subentries. *Sub* means "under" or "below." *Sub* is a prefix added at the beginning of some words. A prefix changes the meaning of a word. Subentries are words that come below an entry word.

At the top of the next column is a part of an index from another book. Find the entry words and the subentries. They are labeled to help you find them easily.

ENTRY	Fish
SUBENTRIES	and Lake Erie, 138
	in Netherlands, 78
ENTRY	Fishing, 78, 127
ENTRY	Floods
SUBENTRIES	in Netherlands, 66
	prevention of, 68,
	134–135

Under the entry word *Fish*, notice the two subentries. The first one is *and Lake Erie, 138*. This means that on page 138 you could find out about fish in Lake Erie.

SKILLS PRACTICE

Let us practice using an index now. The Index in your social studies book begins on page 240. Read the questions below and write your answers on a sheet of paper.

1. On what index page are the words that begin with *O*?
2. On what pages could you find information about oil?
3. On what pages could you find information about electricity?
4. How many subentries are there under *Cities*?
5. Where do you find the list of pages on natural resources: with the words beginning with *N* or with the words beginning with *R*?

3/UNIT REVIEW

1. Everyone needs and uses the products of farms and ranches. — *How many different farm and ranch products do you and your family use during a day? Make a chart showing these products. Give your chart a title.*

2. Today many farmers and ranchers use machines to help them do their work. — *In what way do combines help wheat farmers? How do milking machines help dairy farmers? What machines do many ranchers use today that they did not have years ago?*

3. Many farmers use modern farming methods to help them raise more food. — *Why, do you think, are farmers trying to produce more food? How does irrigation help farmers to grow more crops? In what way do greenhouses help farmers to raise more food? Why do citrus farmers use heaters in the orange groves?*

4. The earth is full of many different kinds of natural resources. Natural resources are valuable because people have learned to use them to make a better life. — *What does* natural resource *mean? How many natural resources can you name? Make a list. How do people use each of these resources?*

5. People need to take care of natural resources so that the resources will not be spoiled and wasted. — *How does our air and water sometimes become polluted? What does* conservation *mean? In what ways are people showing that they care about the earth? What can you do to help conservation efforts?*

Citizenship in the United States

Communities Make and Keep Rules

┌─ **VOCABULARY** ─────────────┐
citizen	vote
council	judge
mayor	penalty
government	fine
election	
└──────────────────────────────┘

Rules at home   We live in a world with rules. There are rules for the games we play. There are rules at home. There are rules at school. There are rules in every community.

Who makes the rules at home? Parents or other adults make most of these rules. Some of the rules in your house may be like the ones shown below. Read each rule. What do you think is the purpose of each rule?

Rules of the House

1. No running inside.
2. Do not throw anything.
3. Leave dirty shoes outside.
4. Do not play on the stairs.
5. Do not play with matches.
6. Put toys away at night.
7. Brush your teeth before going to bed.

Most rules are made to keep people or things safe from harm. Which of the rules were made to protect people? Which were made to protect property, or things that you own?

Rules in the community Almost all communities have rules. These rules are called laws. The **citizens** of a community have a duty to obey the laws.

Wherever you go in a city or a town, you see signs showing some of these laws. There are traffic signs that say Stop and One Way. There are other signs that say No Parking and Keep Off the Grass. Why do communities have these laws?

A soccer game is played according to a set of rules. What, do you think, would happen if the players did not follow the rules?

Who makes community laws? Laws in a community are made by the leaders of the community. In different communities these leaders are called by different names. In many communities the leaders are members of the town **council** or the city council. A council is a group of men and women who are chosen by the people in a community. They are chosen to make laws and plans for the city or town.

In most communities there is a **mayor.** The mayor's job is to see that the laws are carried out. The mayor also works with the council members to help make the laws.

The mayor and the council members are part of the **government** of the community. A government is a group of men and women who make the laws and see that the laws are carried out.

These men and women are members of a town council. They have been elected by the citizens of their community. It is the responsibility of the council to make laws and plans for the community.

Choosing community leaders
In the United States people choose their leaders. They make their choices in an **election.** In an election people **vote,** or say whom they would like to have as a leader. The person who gets the most votes is the one who wins the election. Voting is one part of citizenship.

Keeping the laws Every person in the community has an important job. That job is to obey the laws of the community.

Some people do not obey these laws. This is why communities need police officers. The women and men who work for the police department protect the people from those who break the laws.

When someone has broken a law, it is the job of the police officer to bring that person before a **judge.** The judge listens to those who say that a law was broken and to those who say that a law was not broken. The judge must be fair and hear all sides of the case. If the judge decides that the person disobeyed a law, then

A judge has the responsibility to hear and decide cases in a court of law.

the judge also has to decide on a **penalty** for the person. A penalty is a punishment. There are different penalties for breaking different laws. A person may have to pay a **fine.** This is a certain amount of money that must be paid for not obeying a law. Sometimes the person is put in jail as a penalty.

CHECKUP

1. Why are rules made?
2. What are laws?
3. How do people choose their leaders?
4. Describe the work of a judge.

Communities Provide Services

The need for community services Every day, people depend on certain things. They depend on good streets when they drive to work or to the store. They depend on police and fire departments to help keep them safe. They depend on schools and teachers to help children learn. People in a community need these services and many others. Services are kinds of work that help people.

Most people cannot afford to buy their own fire truck. They cannot afford to build their own schools and streets. This is why most communities provide these needed services.

It takes many workers to provide community services. You know about the work a teacher does. You have read about the work done by police officers and firefighters. Now let us read how some other community workers help people. You may have seen these workers in your community.

Firefighters provide one of the most important services in a community. They risk their lives to save people and protect property from fire.

Machinery helps these road workers tear up a street. Later the workers will put down a new road surface.

Road repair "My name is Jim Morris. It is my job to repair the streets and roads in my community.

"I work with two other people. Each morning we load our truck with blacktop. Blacktop is a material made from coal. We use it to fill in the holes in the roads.

"When we start working on a street, we have to be careful. We put signs out all along the road to tell drivers that we are working. We also wear brightly colored shirts and hats to help drivers see us.

"Sometimes there are too many holes to fill. Then we repave the street. The paving truck spreads blacktop all over the street. Then we drive a roller machine over the new blacktop. The machine rolls the blacktop until it is smooth and hard.

"Besides repairing roads, my job includes painting new lines on roads. I also clear ice and snow from roads in winter."

Library service "I am Angela Gendusa. I work as a librarian in my community library.

"People will find many useful things in our library. We have newspapers and magazines, as well as books. We also have records, filmstrips, and pictures. Anyone who has our library card may borrow our materials. You may get a library card if you live in the community. To get a card, you have to fill out a form and sign it. If you are a child, your mother or father must sign it, too.

The card catalog tells a student whether the library has the book she needs.

Librarians help people find the information they need for work or school.

"The library is open six days a week. It is also open a few nights a week. This gives everyone a chance to use the library.

"I spend most of my time helping people find the books they want. I also help people find information they need for work or school.

"Sometimes I show people how to use the **card catalog.** This is a listing of all the books in the library. The cards are in drawers marked with the letters of the alphabet. The cards tell people three things about a book. They tell the name or title, the author's name, and what the book is about."

Parks and recreation department "My name is Pam Weil. I work for the parks and **recreation** (rek rē ā′ shən) department in my community. My job is to help plan recreation, or games and sports.

"The people who work in this department want our parks to be used. We set up swimming programs in summer. We also set up baseball and soccer teams. Many teams play on our fields every day.

"I teach classes of young people. I show them how to play many sports. Last Saturday we had classes in tennis and archery. In tennis you have to learn how to hit a tennis ball over the net. In archery you have to learn how to use a bow and arrow and to shoot carefully at a target.

"There are many different things to do in our parks. We hope more people will want to use our parks more often."

Some communities set up a sports program for the children in the area. Do you have a favorite sport or game that you like to play?

There are usually thousands of animals at a zoo. It takes many workers to feed and care for all the animals.

Working at the zoo "Hi! I am Martin Steele. I work at the zoo in my community. We have more than 3,000 animals. People from all over the state visit our zoo. They see beautiful animals here.

"I spend most of my time in the Children's Zoo. Here you may pet some of the animals. We have deer, goats, and a baby elephant for children to pet.

"There is a nursery in the Children's Zoo. Most of the baby animals are kept here. Doctors take care of these animals. We want to be sure the baby animals are strong before we let them out of the nursery. When you come to the zoo, be sure to see the nursery. You may even see me feeding a baby animal with a bottle."

Who pays for community services? It takes a lot of money to provide community services. The many people who work for the community have to be paid. Places such as parks and zoos must be kept clean. Buildings such as schools and libraries must have heat and electricity. Fire trucks, police cars, and school buses must all be kept in good repair. Who pays for all these things? Everyone in the community pays for these services. We all pay because we are all helped by the services.

The money people pay to the city or town is called a **tax.** Taxes are used to pay for many different community services. Most of the tax money comes from people who own land, houses, and other buildings in the community. The owners of the land and buildings pay a **property tax.** The amount of the tax depends on how much the property is worth. If your house is worth more than your neighbor's house, then you must pay more property tax than your neighbor pays.

Money raised through taxes paid to repair this pool for summer swimming.

People can enjoy ice-skating all year round at this rink. The building was given to the community by a large company in the area.

Gifts to a community

Sometimes people give land or buildings to a community. Do you remember reading about Memorial Park in Houston, Texas? This is the park where the trail riders spend the night before the rodeo parade into Houston. The land for the park was given to the city of Houston years ago. The family that gave the land said it could only be used as a park for all the people to enjoy. The land cannot be used for any other purpose.

Other families in the United States have built libraries. Some have built beautiful water fountains. Others have given communities such things as statues and paintings. Has someone in your community made a gift to your city or town?

CHECKUP

1. Why do most communities provide many different services?
2. What kinds of things can you find in a library?
3. What is a property tax?
4. Name some things that people have given to their communities.

Washington, D.C.—Our Capital City

┌─VOCABULARY─────────────┐
litter   memorial
White House   Capitol
monument   astronaut
└────────────────────────┘

Fifty state governments In Chapter 1 you learned that your community is part of a state. You also learned that there are 50 states in the United States. Each state has its own government. The leaders of the state make laws to help and to protect all the people in the state.

There are state traffic laws telling people how to drive their cars safely. There are state school laws telling boys and girls how many years they must go to school. The laws also tell the schools how many days they must be open each year. There are state laws telling people not to throw **litter** on parks and highways. Litter is papers, cans, bottles, and other trash left lying about on the ground. There are state laws telling people not to pollute the air and water. People who are caught breaking these laws may be fined an amount of money or may even be sent to jail.

State capitals State leaders meet to make laws in a special city. This is the state capital. There are 50 state capitals. Look at the map of the United States on pages 16−17. The key shows a symbol for state capitals. What is the capital of your state?

The national capital On the same map of the United States, there is a special symbol. It is for Washington, D.C. This city is the capital of our country, or nation.

Many government buildings in Washington, D.C., are brightly lighted at night.

President Ronald Reagan speaks to members of the Retired Senior Volunteer Program.
These older Americans offer many services to their communities.

Washington is where the government of the United States meets to make laws and plans for all Americans.

Washington, D.C., was named for George Washington. He was the first President of the United States. The President is the leader of the country.

Washington is the only city in the United States that is not in a state. Look again at the map on pages 16–17. You can see that Washington is between Maryland and Virginia. But it is not a part of either state. Washington, D.C., is in the District of Columbia. The city is built on land given to the United States by Maryland. Washington, D.C., was planned as a government city.

A tour of the capital city
There are many interesting places to visit in Washington, D.C. There are too many to see in one day. To help you know more about the capital, let us take a tour. We will visit some of the famous and important places

that most visitors see. Our guides are two high school students from Washington.

Carl: Washington, D.C., is a very beautiful city. Irene and I are proud to live and to go to school here.

Irene: The first place we will visit on our tour is the **White House.** This is where the President of the United States lives. The President's office is here, too. The White House has 132 rooms. It also has a large yard that covers 18 acres (8 ha).

Carl: We can see five of the rooms in the White House. These are the only ones open to visitors. We cannot visit the rooms where the President lives and works.

Irene: Our next stop is a famous **monument** (mon' yə mənt). It is the Washington Monument. It was built to help people remember George Washington. We can take an elevator to the top of the Washington Monument. From there, we can see most of the city.

(Left) The White House is surrounded by beautiful lawns and gardens. (Right) Hockey players skate on the frozen Reflecting Pool in front of the Washington Monument.

Carl: We are going now to the Jefferson Memorial. A **memorial,** like a monument, is built so that people remember someone or something.

Irene: In the Jefferson Memorial is a huge statue of a very famous American. It is President Thomas Jefferson. He was President more than 175 years ago. He helped to guide our new nation through its early years.

Carl: From here we are going to the **Capitol.** This is the main building where the men and women of Congress work. If we are lucky, we may see some of our government leaders on the steps of the Capitol.

Irene: Here we are now at the National Air and Space Museum. We can see the airplane flown by the Wright Brothers. It is hanging from the ceiling. It was the first plane that ever flew. The *Spirit of St. Louis* is here, too. It was the first plane to fly from New York City to Paris, France.

(Left) If you look closely at the Jefferson Memorial, you can see the statue of President Jefferson in the center of the building. (Right) The Capitol is where Congress meets and makes laws for our nation.

At the National Air and Space Museum visitors look at a model of a spacecraft.

Carl: Now we are at the FBI building. FBI stands for Federal Bureau of Investigation. The men and women who work for the FBI are called special agents. They are carefully trained in their work. The FBI investigates, or searches into, more than 180 kinds of crimes. Some of the crimes are kidnapping, bank robbery, and attacking the President.

Carl: In this museum you can also see different spacecraft used by the **astronauts** (as′ trə nôts). An astronaut is an American pilot or scientist who travels and works in space. At the museum you can touch rocks that the astronauts brought back from the moon.

Irene: A few blocks away is the Library of Congress. This is probably the largest library in the world. The members of Congress use this library to get the information they need to make laws. There are many old and valuable books here.

The FBI has a huge collection of fingerprints. It uses computers to keep track of the prints.

Irene: We are going to leave the city of Washington to visit some important places just across the Potomac (pə tō′ mək) River in Virginia. The first place we will visit is the Pentagon. It is the largest office building in the world. It covers 29 acres (12 ha). Amost 27,000 people work here. In the Pentagon are the main offices for our Army, Navy, and Air Force.

Carl: Not far from the Pentagon is Arlington National Cemetery. Thousands of people are buried here. Each of them has served in the United States Army, Navy, or Air Force. President John F. Kennedy is buried here. He once served in the Navy.

This is the grave of President John F. Kennedy at Arlington National Cemetery. An eternal flame burns over the President's grave.

Mount Vernon was George Washington's home on the banks of the Potomac River. Each year more than a million people visit this famous home.

Irene: Our last stop in Virginia is Mount Vernon. This was the home of George Washington. His grave and many of his belongings are here. Mount Vernon looks out on the Potomac River.

Carl: The last place we will visit on this tour is back in Washington. It is the Bureau of Engraving and Printing. Our money is printed here. The person you see over there is checking some new ten-dollar bills.

Irene: In the capital there are many interesting places to visit.

You can see some of the most interesting places in Washington on the drawing on pages 182–183.

CHECKUP

1. How is Washington, D.C., different from any other city in the United States?
2. What is the White House?
3. In what way are a monument and a memorial alike?
4. What happens at the Bureau of Engraving and Printing?

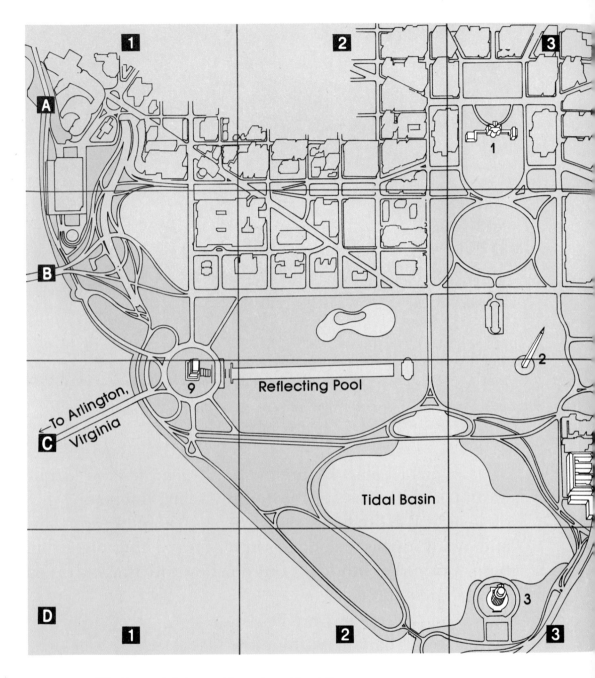

To Arlington, Virginia

Reflecting Pool

Tidal Basin

This drawing of Washington, D.C., has a grid, or system of lines, letters, and numbers. The purpose of a grid is to help you find places. Notice that the lines form boxes as they cross one another on the drawing. Each box is identified by a letter and a number. For example, the box at the upper left of the drawing is **A** **1** . The drawing also has a key that lists some places in Washington. The name of each place has a letter and a number after it. The letter and number tell you where to find that place on the drawing. The White House is in box **A** **3** . Locate the White House on the drawing. Now locate the other places shown in the key.

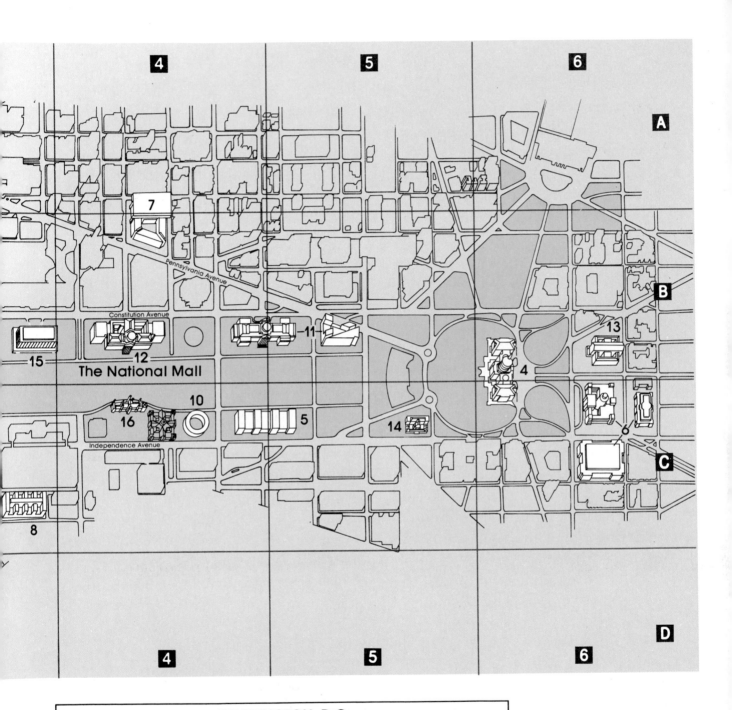

WASHINGTON, D.C.

1 White House **A 3**
2 Washington Monument **C 3**
3 Jefferson Memorial **D 3**
4 United States Capitol **B 6**
5 National Air and Space Museum **C 5**
6 Library of Congress **C 6**
7 Federal Bureau of Investigation **A 4**
8 Bureau of Engraving and Printing **C 3**

9 Lincoln Memorial **C 1**
10 Hirschhorn Museum and Sculpture Garden **C 4**
11 National Gallery of Art **B 5**
12 National Museum of Natural History **B 4**
13 Supreme Court Building **B 6**
14 United States Botanic Garden **C 5**
15 National Museum of History and Technology **B 3**
16 Smithsonian Institution Building **C 4**

KEY FACTS

1. Laws are made by the leaders of a community, state, or nation.

2. The American people choose their leaders by voting for them.

3. Communities provide many needed services.

4. The people in a community pay taxes. Tax money is used to pay for community services.

5. The leaders of state government meet to make laws in the state capital.

6. Washington, D.C., is the capital of the United States.

VOCABULARY QUIZ

Write the numbers 1 to 5 on a sheet of paper. Read each sentence below and decide whether it is true or false. The underlined words are vocabulary terms. Write **T** if the sentence is true and **F** if it is false.

1. A fine is an amount of money that must be paid for not obeying a law.

2. A mayor is the leader of a state.

3. A card catalog is a list of all the birthday cards in a store.

4. A judge is someone who decides whether or not a law has been broken.

5. Litter is trash that people leave lying about on the ground.

REVIEW QUESTIONS

1. Who makes the laws in most communities? Who helps to keep the laws in most communities?

2. What is government?

3. Name some of the services that a community might provide.

4. Who pays for community services?

5. What are some laws that a state government might make?

6. How is the national capital different from state capitals?

7. Describe at least five famous and important places in Washington, D.C.

ACTIVITIES

1. Make a list of the rules you follow at school. Beside each rule write the penalty for breaking the rule.

2. Make a sign that tells other people about a rule in your school. Use drawings, words, or symbols in your sign. Just be sure that other boys and girls understand what your sign means.

3. Read a library book about George Washington, Thomas Jefferson, or another President of the United States. Tell the pupils in your class some of the interesting things you have learned about that President.

READING A MILEAGE CHART

MEASURING DISTANCE

A map scale is one way to find out how far one place is from another. A second way is to use a mileage chart. A mileage chart is usually found on a road map. It helps a map reader find the number of miles between places.

HOW TO READ A MILEAGE CHART

Look at the chart below. Place a finger on *Los Angeles* on the side of the chart. Now place another finger on *San Francisco* at the top of the chart. Move both fingers, one across and the other down, until they meet. Did they meet at 414? That is about the number of road miles between the two cities.

SKILLS PRACTICE

Now do the same for the cities listed below. Number from 1 to 5 and write the correct number of miles between the two cities.

1. Detroit and Miami
2. New York and Washington, D.C.
3. St. Louis and Denver
4. Atlanta and San Antonio
5. Chicago and Houston

MILEAGE CHART	Atlanta	Boston	Chicago	Denver	Detroit	Houston	Los Angeles	Miami	New York	Philadelphia	St. Louis	San Antonio	San Francisco	Washington, D.C.
Atlanta		1036	712	1430	925	791	2236	663	854	748	565	1066	2483	618
Chicago	712	1004		1021	275	1091	2048	1423	809	785	289	1265	2173	709
Detroit	925	662	275	1329		1323	2288	1422	649	577	534	1531	2516	516
Los Angeles	2236	3017	2048	1031	2288	1582		2769	2794	2779	1819	1387	414	2646
New York	854	208	809	1758	649	1827	2794	1279		99	976	1841	2930	237
St. Louis	565	750	289	863	534	837	1819	1226	976	904		977	2118	856
San Francisco	2483	2975	2173	1255	2516	1961	414	3093	2930	3004	2118	1843		2878
Washington, D.C.	618	448	709	1717	516	1365	2646	1043	237	131	856	1627	2878	

Telephone, Radio, and Television

┌─ VOCABULARY ─────────────────┐
communication   satellite
invent   antenna
cable
└──────────────────────────────┘

Learning about our world
In this book you have read about people and communities in many parts of the United States. No matter where they live, most people today know a good deal about the rest of the world. One reason for this is transportation. As you have learned, air, land, and water transportation carry people and products to nearby communities and to faraway countries.

Communication (kə myü nə kā′ shən) is another reason why people know more about the world they live in. *Communication* means "the giving and receiving of information and ideas."

We communicate when we talk and listen to one another. We also communicate when we write and draw. The pictures on the opposite page show ways people communicate. How are the people giving and receiving information?

Communication helps us learn about what is happening in our community, our country, and other parts of the world. We can learn about important events as they take place or very soon afterwards. For example, we can see and hear the President of the United States speaking on television. We can read in the newspaper about the volcano at Mount St. Helens in the state of Washington. We can read in a magazine about the problems facing farmers because of too little rainfall. We can hear on the radio about a traffic jam on the

Communication helps people learn about events in their communities, their nation, and other parts of the world.

highway. We can use the telephone to talk with people around the world. These kinds of communication help us know and understand more about the world we live in.

Changes in communication People have always needed to communicate and share ideas. Long ago people had only a few ways to communicate. They could talk with each other or write letters. There were no radios, televisions, or telephones until people **invented** them. *Invent* means "to make something that no one else has ever made."

Some people have always searched for new and better ways to share information. Their inventions have changed the ways in which we communicate today. Look at the time line below. It shows when some important things have happened in the field of communications.

Using the telephone One of the most important inventions in the field of communications was the telephone. From the time line, you can see that the telephone was invented in 1876. The inventor was Alexander Graham Bell. Mr. Bell did not invent the telephone overnight. It took many months of trying and failing before he got his invention working successfully. Today there are more than 425 million telephones throughout the world.

When was the first daily newspaper published in the United States?

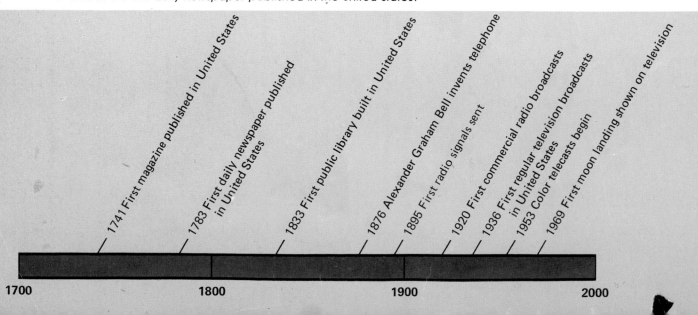

1741 First magazine published in United States

1783 First daily newspaper published in United States

1833 First public library built in United States

1876 Alexander Graham Bell invents telephone

1895 First radio signals sent

1920 First commercial radio broadcasts

1936 First regular television broadcasts in United States

1953 Color telecasts begin

1969 First moon landing shown on television

1700   1800   1900   2000

In 1892 Alexander Graham Bell opened the first long-distance line between New York and Chicago.

"Many years ago," Mr. Ashad continued, "you had to call and tell the operator the name of the person you wanted to talk to. The operator then connected your phone line to the line of the person you were calling.

"Now you can usually pick up your telephone and call almost anywhere in the world without the help of an operator. Today operators only aid those people who need special help in making phone calls.

How does the telephone work? This was a question that Mrs. Reilly's class especially wanted to answer. Mrs. Reilly arranged for the girls and boys to visit the telephone company. There they saw the modern equipment that helps our telephones work.

Mr. Ashad welcomed the class to the telephone company. He explained, "Most of your calls come through our company. The phone lines from the houses in this area come to this building.

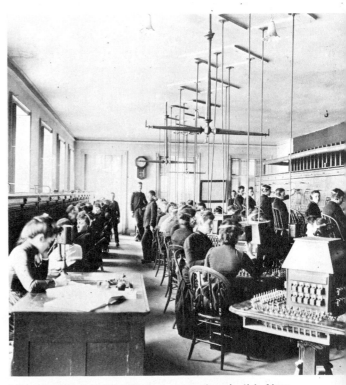

Men and women worked as operators in this New York City telephone office in 1885.

Modern telephone equipment makes it possible to call almost anywhere in the world.

"Within the past twenty years, **satellites** (sat' ə līts) have been used to communicate with people in other countries. A satellite is an object that circles the planet earth carrying communications equipment. Giant rockets place the satellite thousands of miles in space above the earth. On the ground, special stations send signals to the satellite. The satellite sends the signals back to stations in another country.

"You can see that telephone communication has changed," said Mr. Ashad. "In your lifetime, there will probably be many other changes."

"You can call people living in other countries," Mr. Ashad said. "About thirty years ago, a telephone line, or **cable**, was placed on the bottom of the Atlantic Ocean. A cable is a bundle of wires protected by a strong covering. The Atlantic cable let us call people in Europe for the first time. Other cables were placed in the Pacific Ocean. These cables let us call Hawaii and Japan.

How does a communications satellite work?

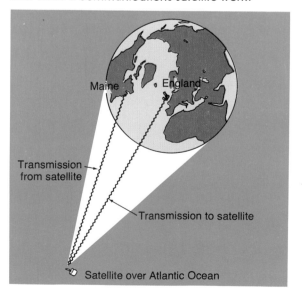

Maine
England
Transmission from satellite
Transmission to satellite
Satellite over Atlantic Ocean

A magic box   To some people, a radio might seem like a magic box. It would seem like magic to you if you did not know what it was. Just imagine finding a box that talks, sings, and makes strange sounds. Today we know what a radio is. Most people in the United States listen to a radio for at least a few minutes every day.

Unlike a telephone, a radio is not connected by a wire to an office or a radio station. A radio has a special **antenna** (an ten′ ə). This is a wire or a metal rod that picks up radio waves or signals. The signals are sent out by radio stations. The radio changes these signals that we cannot hear into sounds that we can hear and understand.

Many inventors helped to bring about the invention of the radio. One was an inventor who lived in the country of Italy. His name was Guglielmo (gü lyel′ mō) Marconi (mar kō′ nē). Marconi invented a way of sending radio signals through the air. This happened in 1895. The radio was the first invention that let people hear about events as they took place.

Tall antennas outside this station send radio signals out into the air. The signals are picked up by small wire antennas on radio sets.

Through television, we can see a fire in San Francisco as it happens. Or we can watch a tennis match as it is being played.

Pictures and sounds from around the world   As you can see from the time line on page 188, television is one of the newer means of communication. It is also one of the most important. The word *television* is made up from two other words. The Greek word *tele* means "far." The Latin word *videre* means "to see." So the word *television* means "to see far." Television brings pictures and sounds from around the world into our homes.

In many ways, television is like radio. A television uses an antenna to receive the signal sent out by the television station. The television set changes the signal into pictures that we see and sounds that we hear.

Today most Americans have a television. Of every 100 homes in the United States, 97 homes have television sets. In each of these homes, people use their television for about 6 hours a day.

Television helps us learn about faraway places. We can see and hear the leader of another country on a news show. We can watch a special show about life in Mexico or Canada or China. Television also entertains us. We can watch a movie or see a sports event on television. There are many different shows to enjoy.

CHECKUP

1. What is communication?
2. Who invented the telephone?
3. How are radio and television alike? How are they different?

Newspapers, Magazines, and Books

Communication through print

Print is an important means of communication. *Print* means "the words stamped in ink on paper." Whenever people read a book, a **newspaper,** or a **magazine,** they are getting information through print.

Newspapers

More than 60 million people read newspapers every day in the United States. A newspaper is made up of sheets of paper on which are printed news stories. There are also ads and other useful information.

Most newspapers are printed every day. They are called daily newspapers. There are about 1,800 daily papers in the United States. Many large communities have more than one daily paper. You may read a newspaper that is printed in the morning or one that is printed in the evening. A daily newspaper tells us what is happening in the world, in our country, and in our community. The most important news of the day is given on the front page of the paper.

Some newspapers are printed once a week. They are called

Stacks of daily newspapers are delivered to newsstands throughout the country. Millions of Americans read newspapers every day.

weekly newspapers. They are usually printed in the suburbs of large cities or in small towns. A weekly paper has news of special interest to the people in one community.

There are a number of steps in producing a newspaper. One of the most important steps is gathering the news. This is the job of a **reporter.** A reporter interviews people to gather information for a news story. Sometimes a reporter has to research, or search out, facts for a story. The reporter does this to be sure the information is true. The facts must be correct because millions of readers depend on newspapers for information.

Magazines   When was the last time you were in a store and saw racks or shelves filled with magazines? A magazine is a collection of stories or articles. Most magazines have bright covers. The cover shows a picture and the name of the magazine. It also tells something about the stories in the magazine. Look at the magazine covers on page 195.

Each year several thousand different magazines are printed in the United States. Some of them are printed every week. Other magazines are printed every month or every few months.

Magazines give us information and ideas about many different things. Magazines like *Time, Newsweek,* and *U.S. News & World Report* are news magazines. They are printed each week and have articles that explain the news of the week. Articles in magazines often give readers more details about an event than newspaper articles give.

Some magazines are written for one group of people. There are magazines written for boys and girls in elementary school. Some of those magazines are *American Girl, Boys' Life, Jack & Jill, Ranger Rick's Nature Magazine, Highlights for Children,* and *National Geographic World.*

Many magazines have articles on one or two special subjects. What would you learn about if you read *Flying, Golf Digest, Field & Stream, Skiing,* or *Better Homes and Gardens?*

What subjects would you learn about from the magazines shown here?

Most magazines have a **table of contents.** This tells you the names of the articles in the magazine and the pages on which the articles may be found.

Books All books, including your school books, are a form of communication. By reading this social studies book, you have learned about many communities in the United States. You have probably read other books at home. From each book, you receive information and ideas. Sometimes you learn something new. Other times you learn more about a subject.

195

You may borrow many interesting books from the public library. Do you have a library card?

Books are one way that a person can communicate with many other people. The author of this book lives in Texas, but the book will be read by pupils in every state and in several countries.

CHECKUP

1. Name three examples of communication through print.
2. In what ways are daily newspapers different from weekly newspapers?
3. What is the job of a reporter?
4. How is a news magazine different from a newspaper?
5. What is the purpose of the table of contents?

Letters

┌─ **VOCABULARY** ─────────────────┐

ZIP code   **solar energy**

└──────────────────────────────────┘

Written communication

One of the oldest forms of communication is letter writing. People have written letters for thousands of years. When you write a letter, you share your thoughts and ideas with someone else. Today you can send a letter to another person almost anywhere in the world.

It is the job of the United States Postal Service to deliver the letters and other mail that people send. There are about 32,000 post offices in our country. At a post office a person can mail a letter or package and buy stamps. The money people pay for stamps is used to run the postal service.

Other countries also have post offices or mail services. You or a friend might collect stamps from faraway places. The picture on page 197 shows postage stamps from several countries.

Can you tell which country each stamp is from? One who collects stamps is a philatelist.

APOLLO 14
Shepard
Roosa
Mitchell
LIBERIA POSTAGE 12c

EXPEDICION DE LA BALSA "ACALI"
21-VIII-73
MEXICO 80¢ AEREO
H. RODRIGUEZ T.I.E.V 1975

6 TARRAGONA
TOAS
S.A.
CORREOS
ESPAÑA

10 H.
POSTAGE
المملكة
العربية
السعودية
K.S.A.

HOMENAGEM AO EMIGRANTE
PORTUGAL 14.00

USA Olympics 1980
15c

EGMONT NATIONAL PARK
New Zealand 23c

Papilio thoas melonius
PAPILIONIDAE
Jamaica 20c

日本郵便
若狭湾国定公園 10

GIANT SEQUOIA
Sequoiadendron giganteum
USA 15c

REPUBLICA DOMINICANA
1c
ASOCIACION
1976
DOMINICANA DE
REHABILITACION

Australia 25c
Wool

Special
Olympics

Skill·Sharing·Joy
USA 15c

NICARAGUA
2 CORDOBAS CORREO
ESCOGIDO POR VOTACIÓN MUNDIAL
FACCHETTI. ITALIA
vasarhelyi

CANADA
POSTES POSTAGE
R.C.M.P.
10 CENTS

Delivering a letter   What do you think happens to a letter when it is mailed? In Chapter 2 you met Miss Teffeau. She is an editor at Silver Burdett Company. Let us follow a letter that Miss Teffeau has written to the author of this book. The author lives in Humble, Texas.

"After I write the letter," Miss Teffeau explains, "I put it in an envelope. On the front of the envelope, I write the author's name and address. I also write my name and address in the upper left-hand corner. Then I place a stamp on the envelope. It shows that I have paid for this letter to be delivered.

"I drop the envelope into a mailbox. Workers for the postal service collect the mail from the mailboxes. They take the mail to a post office. There other workers sort the mail. They put envelopes that are the same size together. The envelopes then go to a machine. It prints the name of the city where the letter was mailed and the date on the envelope. It also marks the stamp. This keeps someone from using a stamp twice.

"Another machine "reads" the **ZIP code** on the envelope. The ZIP code is a group of numbers that are part of the address. These numbers tell where my letter is going. My envelope is put with other letters going to the Houston area.

"Then a truck carries the mail to the airport. At the airport my letter is put on an airplane going to Houston, Texas.

At the post office, letters are put onto a moving belt and then sorted according to the size of the envelope.

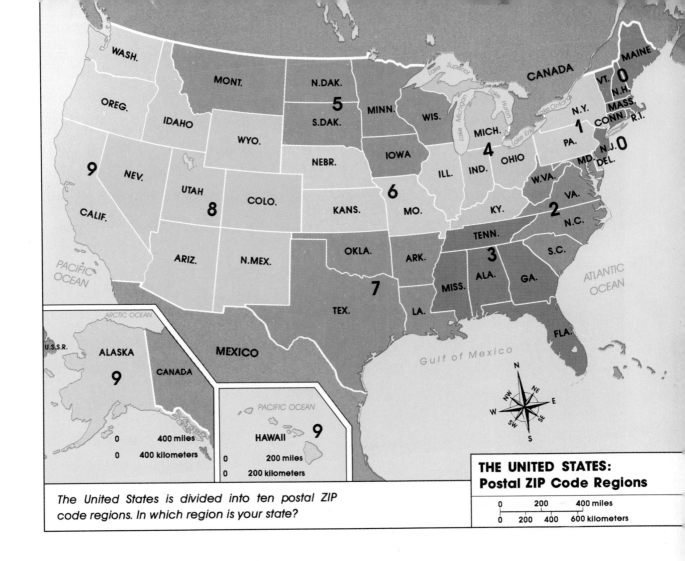

The United States is divided into ten postal ZIP code regions. In which region is your state?

**THE UNITED STATES:
Postal ZIP Code Regions**

"In Houston a mail truck meets the airplane, and workers unload the mailbags. The truck carries the mail to the Houston Post Office. At the post office the mail is sorted by ZIP code. Those envelopes with the same ZIP code are sent to the same city. My envelope is placed together with those showing a ZIP code of 77338. This is the number for Humble, Texas.

"If you look at the map above, I think it will help you see how ZIP codes work. The map shows ten regions, or parts, of the United States. The first number in every ZIP code stands for one of these regions. In the ZIP code 77338, the first number, 7, shows the region of the country where the letter should go. As you can see from the map, that region includes Texas.

"The second and third numbers in the ZIP code show postal areas within the region. You can see the postal areas for Texas by looking at the map below. To find the area where my letter is going, use the first three numbers of the ZIP code—773. Can you find that area on the map?

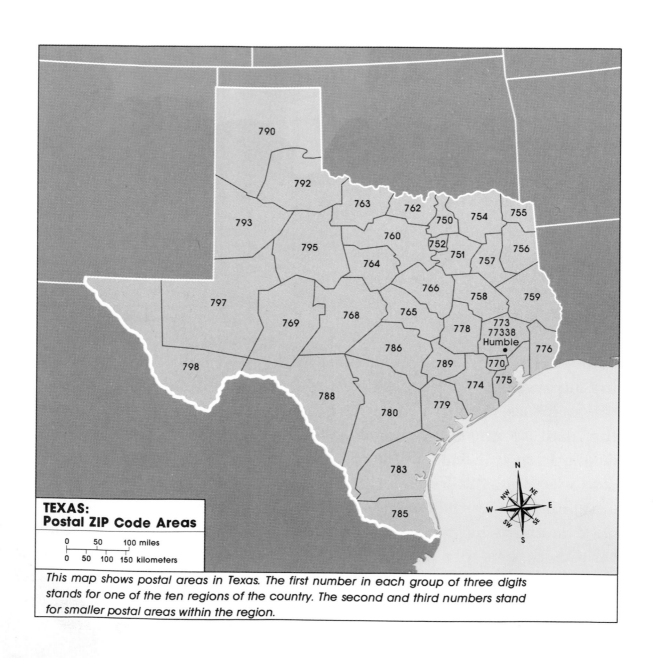

TEXAS:
Postal ZIP Code Areas

0   50   100 miles

0   50   100   150 kilometers

This map shows postal areas in Texas. The first number in each group of three digits stands for one of the ten regions of the country. The second and third numbers stand for smaller postal areas within the region.

A truck carries mail from the airport to the community post office.

"The last two numbers of the ZIP code tell which community post office a letter should be sent to. The numbers 38 mean my letter goes to the post office in Humble. There a letter carrier picks up the mail for the part of town where the author lives. The letter carrier sorts the mail by address and then delivers the mail. My letter to the author is delivered to the correct address. By using the right ZIP code, my letter reaches Humble quickly."

A changing world In this chapter you have read about some important means of communication. You have also learned how communication helps to bring the people of the world closer together. Today news can travel to faraway places in a few seconds. By sharing ideas and information with people, we begin to know them better. We also begin to understand things that are happening in the world around us.

The world as we know it is always changing. People are always trying to invent new products or ways of doing things that may make our lives better. Doctors are working to make us healthier. They are discovering new medicines and ways of treating diseases. Someday we may even be able to take a pill that will keep us from getting a cold.

Scientists are improving our means of communication and transportation. In the future, we may be able to communicate and move from place to place in ways that we have not thought of yet.

Energy from the sun is used to heat this school building. The large solar panels on the roof trap the sunlight and make heat.

New ways of building houses, offices, and stores will be developed. More and more houses may be heated by **solar energy,** or power from the sun. Large solar panels on the roof of a house will be heated by the sun. These panels will then help to heat the house. Solar energy may be one way to conserve on our use of oil.

After many weeks, you have come to the end of your social studies book. But you have not come to the end of learning about the world you live in. All of your life you will be asking questions, searching for answers, and learning about your world.

CHECKUP

1. Why do you think you should write your own address on letters that you send?
2. Why are stamps used?
3. How do ZIP codes help the delivery of the mail?
4. What is solar energy?

KEY FACTS

1. Modern communication helps us learn about events in our city or town, our nation, and the world.

2. The telephone allows people to talk with others who live far away.

3. The radio was the first invention to let people hear about distant events as they happened.

4. Television lets us see and hear about other people, places, and events.

5. Newspapers, magazines, and books are important sources of information about the world we live in.

6. Letter writing is one of the oldest forms of communication.

VOCABULARY QUIZ

Write the numbers 1 to 10 on a sheet of paper. Match the words with their meanings below.

a. communication   f. invent
b. newspaper   g. magazine
c. antenna   h. solar energy
d. reporter   i. ZIP code
e. satellite   j. table of contents

1. One who gathers facts for a news story

2. To make something that no one else has ever made

3. An object that circles the earth carrying communications equipment

4. A listing of articles in a magazine

5. Power from the sun

6. A printed collection of articles bound together with a cover

7. A series of numbers used by the postal service to speed up mail delivery

8. The giving and receiving of ideas

9. A wire or metal rod that picks up radio or television signals

10. Sheets of paper printed with the news

REVIEW QUESTIONS

1. What changes have taken place in telephone communications since the first telephone was invented?

2. Why is *television* a good name for that form of communication?

3. Compare modern newspapers and magazines.

4. What does the United States Postal Service do?

ACTIVITIES

1. Write a newspaper article telling about something that has happened at school or in your community.

2. Address an envelope to a friend. Be sure to include the ZIP code. Draw a stamp in the upper right-hand corner of the envelope.

8/SKILLS DEVELOPMENT

WRITING A LETTER

WHAT IS A LETTER?

Letters are written messages. They help us communicate with each other. Letters let us share our thoughts, feelings, news, and other information.

A SPECIAL LETTER

One of the first things you read in this book was a letter. It was titled "A Letter to You from the Author." Please read the letter again. You will find it in the front of the book. As you read the letter, try to answer these questions.

1. To whom is the author writing?
2. Why is the author writing this letter?
3. When does the author tell you his reason for writing?
4. What did you learn from the second paragraph?
5. What is the main idea in the third paragraph? In the fourth paragraph?
6. Why was the last paragraph written?
7. Who is the author of this book?

SKILLS PRACTICE

Now that you have read the author's letter, it is your turn to write a letter to Mr. Loftin. He would like to know a little about the boys and girls who have read his book. He would also like to know what you have learned in social studies this year. To help you write the letter, you might want to use some of the ideas listed below.

1. In the first paragraph, tell why you are writing the letter.
2. In the second paragraph, tell the author about yourself. You might want to include information about where you were born, where you live now, and what you particularly like about your community.
3. In the third paragraph, tell the author about your school, your favorite subjects, and what you especially liked reading about in this book.

When you address the letter, write your name and address in the upper left-hand corner of the envelope. Then write the author's name and address in the center of the envelope. Address the letter to Mr. Loftin at his school address.

Mr. Richard Loftin
Director of Curriculum & Staff Development
Aldine Independent School District
14910 Aldine-Westfield Road
Houston, Texas 77032

4/UNIT REVIEW

1. People live in a world with rules. There are rules at home, at school, and in places of business. — *Why do we have rules? What are some rules in your home? What are some rules in your school? What might happen if you do not follow a rule at home or in school?*

2. Laws are rules that people must obey. Communities, states, and nations all have laws. — *What are some laws that people must obey in your community? Which people in your community help to keep the laws? Describe their jobs. What might happen to someone who breaks the law?*

3. Laws are made by the leaders of a community, state, or nation. — *Who are the leaders in your community? How are these leaders chosen?*

4. Communities provide many needed services. — *What are some services that your community provides? How are these services paid for?*

5. Capital cities are places where our leaders meet to make laws. Each state has a capital. The capital of our nation is Washington, D.C. — *What is the capital of your state? Name some interesting places you might visit in Washington, D.C. What kinds of things would you expect to see at each place? Why is Washington, D.C., the only city in the United States that is not in a state?*

6. Communication, like transportation, has helped to bring the people of the world closer together. — *What does communication mean? How do people communicate? Why is communication important? If we did not have modern ways to communicate, what kind of a world do you think we might live in?*

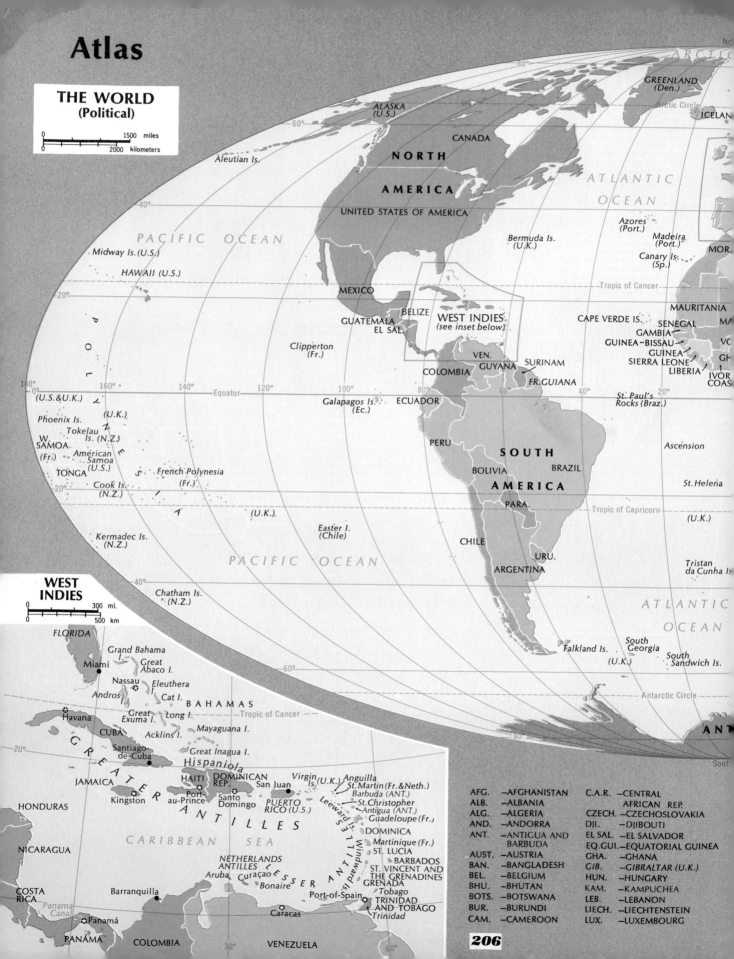

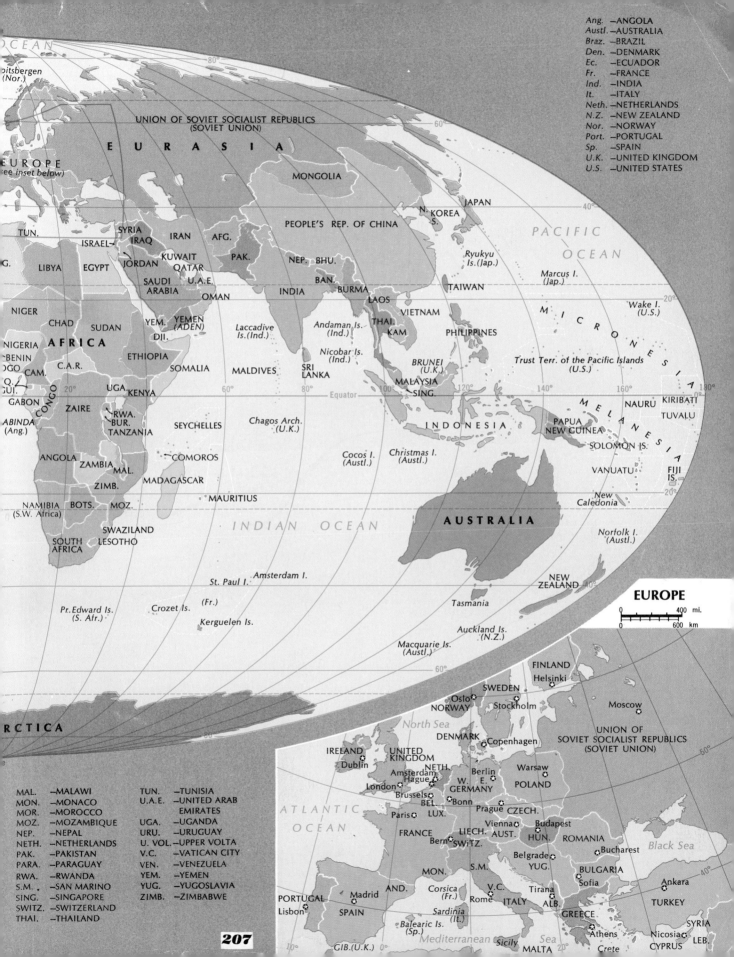

Ang. —ANGOLA
Austl. —AUSTRALIA
Braz. —BRAZIL
Den. —DENMARK
Ec. —ECUADOR
Fr. —FRANCE
Ind. —INDIA
It. —ITALY
Neth. —NETHERLANDS
N.Z. —NEW ZEALAND
Nor. —NORWAY
Port. —PORTUGAL
Sp. —SPAIN
U.K. —UNITED KINGDOM
U.S. —UNITED STATES

OCEAN

pitsbergen
(Nor.)

EUROPE
(see inset below)

EURASIA

UNION OF SOVIET SOCIALIST REPUBLICS
(SOVIET UNION)

MONGOLIA

JAPAN
N. KOREA
S.

PACIFIC
OCEAN

TUN.
SYRIA
IRAQ   IRAN   AFG.
ISRAEL
JORDAN KUWAIT
QATAR
SAUDI U.A.E.
ARABIA
OMAN

PEOPLE'S REP. OF CHINA

Ryukyu
Is.(Jap.)

Marcus I.
(Jap.)

G.
LIBYA   EGYPT

NIGER
CHAD   SUDAN
NIGERIA   AFRICA
BENIN C.A.R.
GO CAM.
GUI.
GABON CONGO ZAIRE
ABINDA
(Ang.)

YEM. YEMEN
DJI. (ADEN)

NEP. BHU.
PAK.
BAN.
INDIA   BURMA
Laccadive
Is.(Ind.)

LAOS
THAI. VIETNAM
KAM

TAIWAN

Wake I.
(U.S.)

M I C R O N E S I A

ETHIOPIA

SOMALIA
MALDIVES
SRI
LANKA

Andaman Is.
(Ind.)

Nicobar Is.
(Ind.)

PHILIPPINES

BRUNEI
(U.K.)
MALAYSIA
SING.

Trust Terr. of the Pacific Islands
(U.S.)

UGA. KENYA
RWA.
BUR.
TANZANIA

SEYCHELLES

Equator

INDONESIA

PAPUA
NEW GUINEA

M E L A N E S I A

NAURU KIRIBATI
TUVALU

ANGOLA ZAMBIA
MAL.
ZIMB.

COMOROS

MADAGASCAR

Chagos Arch.
(U.K.)

Cocos I.
(Austl.)

Christmas I.
(Austl.)

SOLOMON IS.

VANUATU

FIJI
IS.

NAMIBIA BOTS. MOZ.
(S.W. Africa)

MAURITIUS

INDIAN OCEAN

AUSTRALIA

New
Caledonia

SWAZILAND
SOUTH LESOTHO
AFRICA

St. Paul I.

Amsterdam I.

Norfolk I.
(Austl.)

NEW
ZEALAND

Pr. Edward Is.
(S. Afr.)

Crozet Is.

(Fr.)

Kerguelen Is.

Tasmania

Auckland Is.
(N.Z.)

RCTICA

Macquarie Is.
(Austl.)

MAL. —MALAWI
MON. —MONACO
MOR. —MOROCCO
MOZ. —MOZAMBIQUE
NEP. —NEPAL
NETH. —NETHERLANDS
PAK. —PAKISTAN
PARA. —PARAGUAY
RWA. —RWANDA
SING. —SINGAPORE
SWITZ. —SWITZERLAND
THAI. —THAILAND

TUN. —TUNISIA
U.A.E. —UNITED ARAB
          EMIRATES
UGA. —UGANDA
URU. —URUGUAY
U. VOL. —UPPER VOLTA
V.C. —VATICAN CITY
VEN. —VENEZUELA
YEM. —YEMEN
YUG. —YUGOSLAVIA
ZIMB. —ZIMBABWE

EUROPE

0   400 mi.
0   600 km

FINLAND
Helsinki

SWEDEN
Oslo
NORWAY Stockholm

Moscow

North Sea

DENMARK
Copenhagen

UNION OF
SOVIET SOCIALIST REPUBLICS
(SOVIET UNION)

IRELAND UNITED
Dublin KINGDOM
NETH.
Amsterdam
London Hague
Brussels
BEL. Bonn

Berlin
W. E.
GERMANY

Warsaw

POLAND

ATLANTIC
OCEAN

Paris

LUX.

Prague CZECH.

FRANCE

Bern
SWITZ.

Vienna
LIECH. AUST.

Budapest
HUN. ROMANIA

Belgrade
YUG. Bucharest

MON.

S.M.

BULGARIA
Sofia

Ankara

Black Sea

PORTUGAL
Lisbon

Madrid

SPAIN

AND.

Corsica
(Fr.)

V.C.
Rome
Sardinia
(It.)

ITALY

Tirana
ALB.

GREECE

TURKEY

SYRIA

Balearic Is.
(Sp.)

Mediterranean

Sicily

Athens

MALTA

Crete

Nicosia
CYPRUS

LEB.

GIB.(U.K.)

Sea

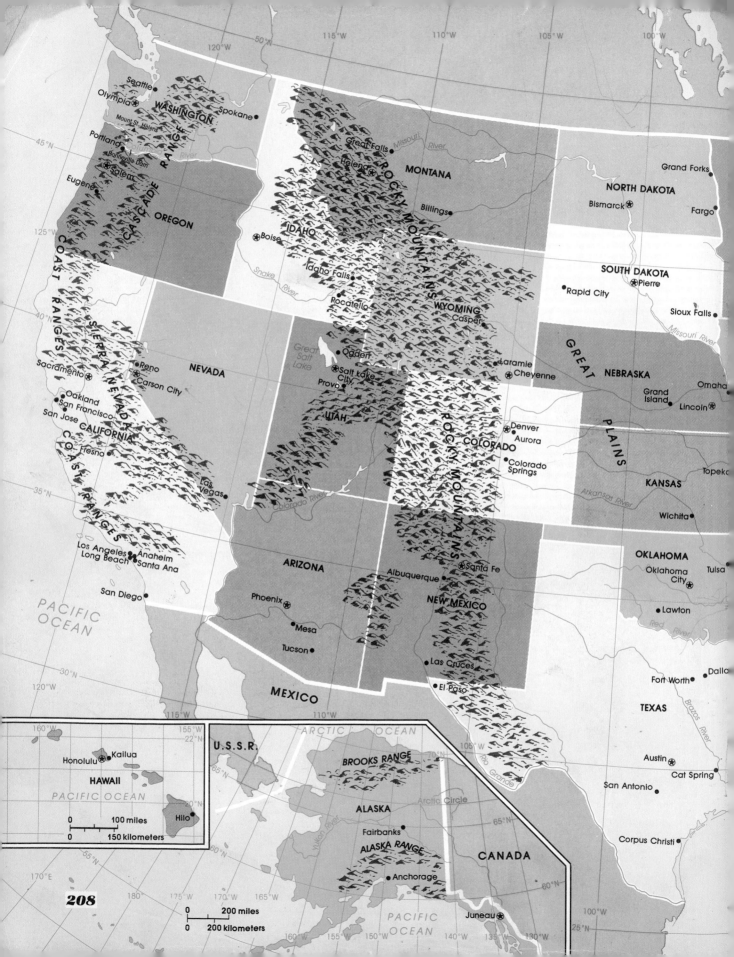

Seattle
Olympia ⊕
WASHINGTON
Spokane
Mount St. Helens ▲
Portland
Bonneville Dam
Salem ⊕
Eugene
OREGON
CASCADE RANGE
COAST RANGES
Sacramento ⊕
Reno
Carson City
NEVADA
Oakland
San Francisco
San Jose
SIERRA NEVADA
CALIFORNIA
Fresno
COAST RANGES
Las Vegas
Los Angeles Anaheim
Long Beach Santa Ana
San Diego

PACIFIC
OCEAN

Great Falls
Helena ⊕
ROCKY MOUNTAINS
MONTANA
Billings
IDAHO
Boise
Idaho Falls
Snake River
Pocatello
WYOMING
Casper
Great Salt Lake
Ogden
Salt Lake City ⊕
Provo
UTAH
Colorado River
ROCKY MOUNTAINS
Laramie
Cheyenne ⊕
Denver
Aurora
COLORADO
Colorado Springs
Santa Fe ⊕
Albuquerque
NEW MEXICO
ARIZONA
Phoenix ⊕
Mesa
Tucson
Las Cruces
El Paso

MEXICO

Missouri River
Grand Forks
NORTH DAKOTA
Bismarck ⊕
Fargo
SOUTH DAKOTA
Rapid City
Pierre ⊕
Sioux Falls
Missouri River
GREAT PLAINS
NEBRASKA
Grand Island
Omaha
Lincoln ⊕
Topeka
KANSAS
Arkansas River
Wichita
OKLAHOMA
Oklahoma City ⊕
Tulsa
Lawton
Red River
Fort Worth
Dallas
TEXAS
Austin ⊕
Cat Spring
San Antonio
Brazos River
Corpus Christi
Rio Grande

HAWAII
160°W
155°W
22°N
Honolulu ⊕ Kailua
HAWAII
PACIFIC OCEAN
20°N
Hilo
0   100 miles
0   150 kilometers

ARCTIC OCEAN
U.S.S.R.
BROOKS RANGE
70°N
Yukon River
Arctic Circle
ALASKA
65°N
Fairbanks
ALASKA RANGE
CANADA
Anchorage
60°N
PACIFIC OCEAN
Juneau ⊕

0   200 miles
0   200 kilometers

CANADA

MINNESOTA
Duluth •

MICH.

St. Paul ⊛
Minneapolis •

WISCONSIN
Green Bay •

Lake Superior

Lake Michigan

Lake Huron

MICHIGAN
Grand
Rapids •
Madison •
Milwaukee •
Lansing ⊛
Detroit •

IOWA
Des
Moines ⊛
Cedar
Rapids •
Rockford •

Chicago •
Gary •
Fort
Wayne •
Toledo •

Lake Erie

Cleveland •

Akron •

ILLINOIS
Springfield ⊛
Indianapolis ⊛

INDIANA

OHIO
Columbus ⊛
Dayton •
Cincinnati •

Lake Ontario
Rochester •
Buffalo •

NEW YORK
Albany ⊛

St. Lawrence River

Burlington •
Montpelier ⊛
Rutland •
VT. **N.H.**
Concord ⊛
Springfield •
MASS.
Worcester •
Boston •
Providence ⊛
CONN. Cranston •
Hartford ⊛ **R.I.** Warwick •
Bridgeport •
New Haven •
Yonkers •
Jersey City •
New York •

Augusta ⊛
Lewiston •
MAINE
Portland •
Nashua •
Manchester •

MOUNTAINS

Scranton •
Newark •

Kansas
City •

Kansas City •
Jefferson City ⊛

St. Louis •

MISSOURI

PENNSYLVANIA
Harrisburg ⊛
Pittsburgh •
Wheeling •

Trenton ⊛
**NEW
JERSEY**
Newark •
Philadelphia •
Wilmington •
Dover ⊛
DELAWARE

ATLANTIC
OCEAN

Louisville •
Frankfort ⊛
Lexington •

KENTUCKY

Ohio River

Huntington •

WEST VIRGINIA
Charleston ⊛

Baltimore •
Rockville •
MD.
Washington
D.C. ⊛
Annapolis ⊛

Richmond ⊛
VIRGINIA

Norfolk •
Virginia Beach •

ARKANSAS
Fort Smith •
North
Little Rock •
Little Rock ⊛

Memphis •

Nashville ⊛

TENNESSEE

Knoxville •

APPALACHIAN

Greensboro •
Raleigh ⊛

NORTH CAROLINA
Charlotte •

**THE UNITED STATES
OF AMERICA**

Key
Rivers
Mountains
⊛ National Capital
⊛ State Capitals
• Other Cities

0   100   200 miles
0   100   200   300 kilometers

MISSISSIPPI
Meridian •
Jackson ⊛

Birmingham •

ALABAMA
Montgomery ⊛

Atlanta ⊛

GEORGIA
Columbus •

SOUTH CAROLINA
Columbia ⊛

North
Charleston •
Charleston •

Shreveport •

LOUISIANA

Biloxi •
Mobile •

Savannah •

Baton Rouge ⊛
New Orleans •
Houston •
Morgan City •

Tallahassee ⊛

Jacksonville •

Gulf of
Mexico

N
NW NE
W   E
SW SE
S

FLORIDA

Tampa •
St. Petersburg •

25°N

Miami • Miami Beach •

75°W

209

ASIA

Bering
Sea

ARCTIC OCEAN

Barrow

Beaufort Sea

Thule

GREENLAND
(Den.)

ICELAND

ALASKA
(U.S.)

Fairbanks

Anchorage

Dawson.

Arctic Circle

Pond
Inlet

Baffin
Bay

Godthaab

Gulf
of
Alaska

Juneau

Port Radium

Great
Bear
Lake

Great Slave
Lake

C A N A D A

Labrador Sea

Hudson
Bay

Churchill

Goose Bay

Edmonton

Calgary

Regina

Lake
Winnipeg

Seven Islands

Gander

PACIFIC
OCEAN

Victoria

Vancouver

Seattle

Spokane

Winnipeg

St. John's

Portland

Columbia

Missouri R.

Quebec

Halifax

San Francisco

Great
Salt
Lake

Salt
Lake
City

U N I T E D   S T A T E S   O F   A M E R I C A

Minneapolis

St. Paul

Milwaukee

Great
Lakes

Montreal

Ottawa

Toronto

Boston

Los Angeles

Denver

Omaha

Chicago

Detroit

Cleveland

Buffalo

New York

Colorado

Kansas
City

St. Louis

Cincinnati

Pittsburgh

Washington

Philadelphia

Baltimore

San Diego

Phoenix

Arkansas R.

Ohio R.

Norfolk

Guadalupe I.
(Mex.)

Memphis

Atlanta

Bermuda Is.
(U.K.)

Tropic of Cancer

G. of California

El Paso

Rio Grande

Dallas

San Antonio

Houston

New
Orleans

ATLANTIC
OCEAN

Monterrey

GULF OF
MEXICO

M E X I C O

Guadalajara

Miami

Grand
Bahama I.

Great Abaco I.

Nassau

Eleuthera I.

Andros
I.

Cat I.

Havana

Gr.
Exuma I.

Long I.

B A H A M A S

Mayaguana I.

Den. —DENMARK
Fr. —FRANCE
Neth.—NETHERLANDS
Mex.—MEXICO
U.K.—UNITED KINGDOM
U.S.—UNITED STATES

Mexico City

Orizaba

CUBA

Acklins I.

Santiago-
de-Cuba

Gr. Inagua I.

DOMINICAN
REPUBLIC

Virgin Is.

(U.S.)

(U.K.)

JAMAICA

HAITI

Port-
au-Prince

Santo
Domingo

PUERTO
RICO

Guadeloupe
(Fr.)

NORTH AMERICA
(Political)

——— International boundaries

✪ National capitals

● Other cities

0 ———————— 500 miles

0 ———————— 800 kilometers

210

Belmopan

BELIZE

GUATEMALA

Guatemala

San Salvador

EL SALVADOR

HONDURAS

Tegucigalpa

Kingston

NICARAGUA

CARIBBEAN
SEA

DOMINICA

Martinique (Fr.)

ST. LUCIA

Neth.
Antilles

ST. VINCENT AND
THE GRENADINES

GRENADA

Managua

San José

Panama
Canal

COSTA RICA

Panamá

PANAMA

TRINIDAD
AND
TOBAGO

SOUTH
AMERICA

West longitude

80° 70° 60° 50° 40°

Barranquilla
Cartagena
Maracaibo
Cúcuta
San Cristóbal
Medellín
Bucaramanga
Bogotá
Cali
COLOMBIA
Valencia
Barquisimeto
Caracas
Port-of-Spain
TRINIDAD AND TOBAGO
VENEZUELA
Orinoco R.
Georgetown
Paramaribo
GUYANA
SURINAM
Cayenne
FRENCH GUIANA (Fr.)

Col. — COLOMBIA
Fr. — FRANCE
U.K. — UNITED KINGDOM

Malpelo I. (Col.)
Quito
ECUADOR
Guayaquil
Iquitos
Equator 0°
Amazon R.
Manaus
Belém
São Luis
Fortaleza

Trujillo
PERU
Callao
Lima
Cuzco
Arequipa
Lake Titicaca
La Paz
BOLIVIA
Sucre
BRAZIL
Recife
Maceió
Brasília (Federal District)
Salvador
10°

Chuquicamata
Antofagasta
PARAGUAY
Asunción
Belo Horizonte
Rio de Janeiro
São Paulo
Niterói
Santos
Tropic of Capricorn
20°

San Felix I. (Chile)
San Ambrosio I. (Chile)
Tucumán
Curitiba
Pôrto Alegre

CHILE
Córdoba
Santa Fe
Paraná
Rosario
URUGUAY
Valparaíso
Santiago
Juan Fernández Is. (Chile)
Buenos Aires
La Plata
Montevideo
Rio de la Plata
ATLANTIC OCEAN
30°

Concepción
ARGENTINA
Mar del Plata
Bahía Blanca

PACIFIC OCEAN

Paraná R.

40°

Falkland Is. (U.K.)

SOUTH AMERICA
(Political)

International boundaries
National capitals
Other cities

0   500 miles
0   800 kilometers

Punta Arenas
Strait of Magellan

211

West longitude

ATLANTIC OCEAN

Madeira Is. (Port.)

PORTUGAL
Lisbon
SPAIN
Madrid
Valencia
Barcelona
Balearic Is. (Sp.)

Bordeaux
FRANCE
Paris
Marseilles
Corsica
Nice
Milan
Sardinia
ITALY
Rome
Naples
Palermo
Sicily
MALTA
Valetta

UNITED KINGDOM
Glasgow
Dublin
IRE.
London
Amsterdam
Brussels
The Hague
Hannover
GER.
E. GER.
Bonn
Munich
Berlin
Prague
Vienna
Budapest
Belgrade
YUG.
Tirana
Athens
GREECE
Crete (Gr.)
Izmir

North Sea
Bergen
Oslo
NORWAY
Göteborg
Copenhagen
DEN.
Hamburg
Stockholm
Helsinki
SWEDEN
FINLAND
Tallinn
Riga
Kaliningrad
POLAND
Warsaw
Wrocław
ROM.
Bucharest
Sofia
BUL.
Istanbul (Constantinople)
Ankara
TURKEY
Nicosia
CYPRUS
Beirut
Jerusalem
ISRAEL
Damascus
SYRIA
Amman
JOR.
Sinai Pen.
Mediterranean Sea

Narvik
Murmansk
Archangel
Leningrad
Moscow
Kiev
Kharkov
Odessa
UKRAINE
Krasnodar
Black Sea
Saratov
Kazan
Perm
Sverdlovsk
Ufa
Chelyabinsk
Kuibyshev
Magnitogorsk
Orenburg
Volga R.
Volgograd
Caspian Sea
Baku
Aral Sea
TURKESTAN
Tashkent
Ob R.

Barents Sea
Spitsbergen (Nor.)
North Land
Novaya Zemlya
ARCTIC OCEAN
Yenisei R.

UNION OF SOVIET (SOVIET UNION)
Omsk
Tomsk
Novosibirsk
Urumchi
SINKIANG

EUROPE
ASIA

BAN. —BANGLADESH
BHU. —BHUTAN
BUL. —BULGARIA
DEN. —DENMARK
GER. —GERMANY
IRE. —IRELAND
JOR. —JORDAN
KAM. —KAMPUCHEA
NEP. —NEPAL
ROM. —ROMANIA
YUG. —YUGOSLAVIA
1—ALBANIA
2—ANDORRA
3—AUSTRIA
4—BAHREIN
5—BELGIUM
6—BRUNEI (U.K.)
7—CZECHOSLOVAKIA
8—HUNGARY
9—KUWAIT
10—LEBANON
11—LIECHTENSTEIN
12—LUXEMBOURG
13—MONACO
14—NETHERLANDS
15—QATAR
16—SAN MARINO
17—SINGAPORE
18—SWITZERLAND

AFRICA
Red Sea
Mecca
SAUDI ARABIA
Riyadh
Manama
Riyadh
Doha
Dubai
UNITED ARAB EMIRATES
Empty Quarter
YEMEN (SANA)
San'a
Aden
Madinat ash Sha'b
YEMEN (ADEN)
Socotra (Yemen [Aden])

IRAQ
Baghdad
Basra
Kuwait
Abadan
Tehran
IRAN (PERSIA)
Tigris R.
Euphrates R.
Kabul
AFGHANISTAN
Islamabad
PAKISTAN
Karachi
Hyderabad
Muscat
OMAN
Arabian Sea

Jammu and Kashmir
Lahore
Delhi
New Delhi
Indus R.
TIBET
NEP.
Katmandu
INDIA
Ganges
Ahmadabad
Bombay
Hyderabad
Madras
Laccadive Is. (Ind.)
MALDIVES
Male
Colombo
SRI LANKA
INDIAN OCEAN

East longitude

212

New Siberian Is.

Aleutian Is. (U.S.)

Bering Sea

S i b e r i a

SOCIALIST REPUBLICS

Krasnoyarsk

Magadán

Kamchatka Pen.

Yakutsk

Lena R.

Sea of Okhotsk

Irkutsk

Amur R.

Khabarovsk

Sakhalin

Sapporo

Kuril Islands (U.S.S.R.)

Ulan Bator

MONGOLIA

INNER MONGOLIA

MANCHURIA

Harbin

Fushun

Vladivostok

Sea of Japan

JAPAN

Tokyo

Yokohama

Shenyang

N. KOREA

Pyongyang

Great Wall

Peking

Dairen

Seoul

S. KOREA

Kyoto

Kobe

Nagoya

Osaka

A

Tientsin

Taiyuan

Tsingtao

Pusan

Kitakyushu

Hwang Ho

Nanking

Shanghai

East China Sea

I

Lanchow

Sian

Wuhan

Yangtze R.

PEOPLE'S REPUBLIC OF CHINA

Chengtu

Chungking

Taipei

Ryukyu Is. (Jap.)

Lhasa

TAIWAN

BHU.

Thimbu

Brahmaputra R.

Kunming

Canton

Macao (Port.)

Hong Kong (U.K.)

AN.

Dacca

Mandalay

BURMA

Hanoi

lcutta

Hue

Da Nang

South China Sea

Manila

PHILIPPINES

Vientiane

LAOS

VIETNAM

ay of

Rangoon

THAILAND

Bangkok

KAM.

Davao

engal

Andaman Is. (Ind.)

Phnom Penh

Ho Chi Minh City

Djajapura

PAPUA NEW GUINEA

Nicobar Is. (Ind.)

Bandar Seri Begawan

6

Manado

IRIAN JAYA

New Guinea

Lae

Port Moresby

M A L A Y S I A

Borneo

Medan

Kuala Lumpur

17

Pontianak

Samarinda

Celebes

Coral Sea

Sumatra

Bandjermasin

Ujung Pandang

I N D O N E S I A

Timor

Arafura Sea

Palembang

Jakarta

Surabaja

Bandung

Java

AUSTRALIA

Gr. —GREECE
Ind. —INDIA
Jap. —JAPAN
Nor. —NORWAY
Port. —PORTUGAL
Sp. —SPAIN
U.K. —UNITED KINGDOM
U.S. —UNITED STATES
U.S.S.R.—SOVIET UNION

PACIFIC OCEAN

EURASIA (Political)

International boundaries

Indefinite or temporary boundaries

National capitals

Other cities

0 — 800 mi.
0 — 1200 km

213

ASIA

ARCTIC OCEAN

Barents Sea

ICELAND
Kópavogur
Reykjavík

Faeroe Is. (Den.)

Shetland Is. (U.K.)

Orkney Is. (U.K.)

Outer Hebrides (U.K.)

Norwegian Sea

NORWAY
Trondheim
Bergen
Oslo

SWEDEN
Stockholm
Göteborg

FINLAND
Tampere
Helsinki
Tallinn

Gulf of Bothnia

Baltic Sea

Riga

Vilnius

Gdansk

Leningrad

Gorki
Yaroslavl
Moscow
Tula

Perm
Izhevsk
Kuibyshev
Ufa
Kazan

UNION OF SOVIET SOCIALIST REPUBLICS (SOVIET UNION)

Voronezh
Saratov
Volgograd

Minsk

Kiev
Kharkov
Dnepropetrovsk
Donetsk
Rostov
Krasnodar
Zaporozhye
Krivoi Rog
Odessa
Crimea

Black Sea

Baku
Tbilisi
Yerevan

Caspian Sea

DENMARK
Copenhagen
Århus

North Sea

UNITED KINGDOM
Glasgow
Belfast
Leeds
Manchester
Sheffield
Liverpool
Birmingham
London

IRELAND
Dublin
Cork

ATLANTIC OCEAN

Bay of Biscay

English Channel

NETHERLANDS
Amsterdam
The Hague
Rotterdam

BELGIUM
Ghent
Antwerp
Brussels

LUXEMBOURG
Luxembourg

Hamburg
Bremen
Hannover
EAST GERMANY
Berlin
Dresden
Leipzig

WEST GERMANY
Essen
Duisburg
Dortmund
Düsseldorf
Cologne
Bonn
Frankfurt
Stuttgart
Munich

POLAND
Poznań
Warsaw
Lodz
Wroclaw

Vistula

CZECHOSLOVAKIA
Prague
Brno
Ostrava

Kraków
Lvov

Dnieper R.

FRANCE
Paris
Lyons
Toulouse
Marseilles
Nice

SWITZ.
Bern
Zurich

LIECHTENSTEIN

AUSTRIA
Vienna
Graz

HUNGARY
Budapest
Miskolc

ROMANIA
Cluj
Timisoara
Bucharest

Danube R.

Belgrade
Zagreb
YUGOSLAVIA
Sarajevo

BULGARIA
Sofia
Plovdiv

Skopje
Salonika

ALBANIA
Tirana
Durrës

GREECE
Athens

Aegean Sea

Adriatic Sea

MONACO

SAN MARINO

VATICAN CITY
Rome

ITALY
Milan
Genoa
Florence
Venice
Naples

Corsica (Fr.)

Sardinia (It.)

Sicily (It.)
Palermo

MALTA
Valletta

Mediterranean Sea

ANDORRA

SPAIN
Madrid
Barcelona
Valencia
Saragossa
Seville

Balearic Is. (Sp.)

PORTUGAL
Oporto
Lisbon

Gibraltar (U.K.)

AFRICA

Tunis

CYPRUS
Nicosia
Limassol

Rhodes (Gr.)

Crete (Gr.)

West Longitude

East Longitude

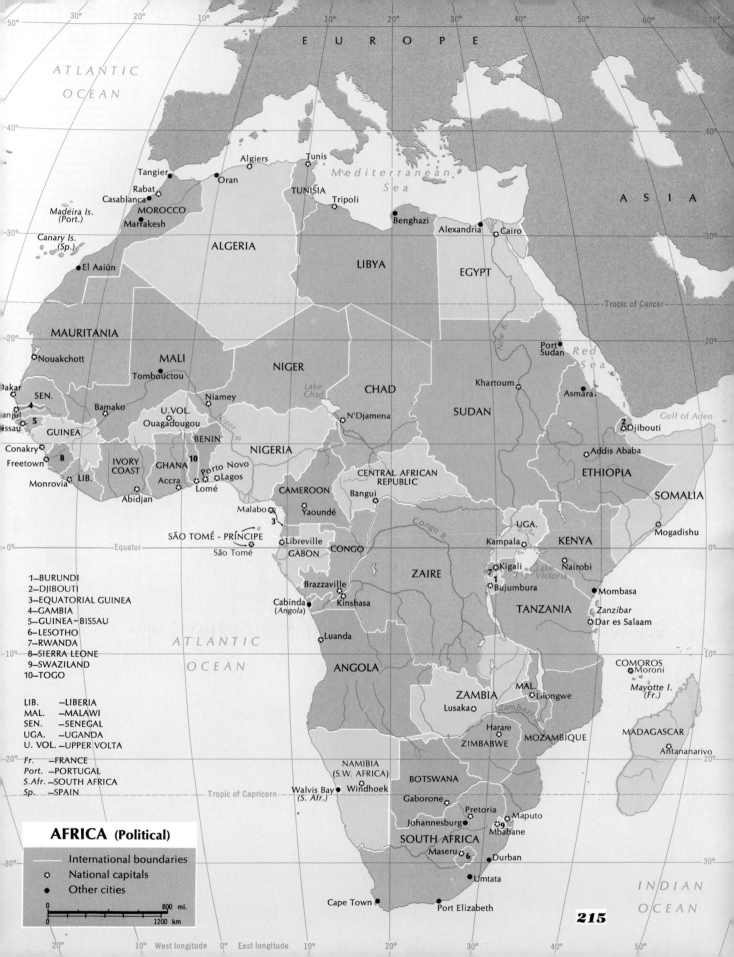

ATLANTIC OCEAN

EUROPE

Madeira Is. (Port.)

Canary Is. (Sp.)

ASIA

Mediterranean Sea

Tangier
Algiers   **Tunis**
Rabat   TUNISIA   Tripoli
Casablanca   **Benghazi**   **Alexandria** **Cairo**
MOROCCO
Marrakesh

ALGERIA   LIBYA   EGYPT

El Aaiún

Tropic of Cancer

MAURITANIA

Port Sudan   Red Sea

Nouakchott   MALI   NIGER   CHAD   SUDAN   **Khartoum**   **Asmara**
Tombouctou   Gulf of Aden
Dakar   Lake Chad   **2** **Djibouti**
SEN.   **Niamey**
4   Bamako   N'Djamena
anjul   U.VOL.   **Addis Ababa**
5   **Ouagadougou**   BENIN
issau   GUINEA   NIGERIA   ETHIOPIA
Conakry   IVORY   GHANA **10**   CENTRAL AFRICAN   SOMALIA
8   COAST   Porto Novo   REPUBLIC
Freetown   **Accra** Lagos   **Bangui**
Monrovia   LIB.   Lomé
Abidjan   CAMEROON   **Mogadishu**
Malabo   **Yaoundé**   UGA.   KENYA
SÃO TOMÉ - PRÍNCIPE   3   **Kampala**
São Tomé   **Libreville**   7 **Kigali**   **Nairobi**
Equator   CONGO   **1** Lake
GABON   ZAIRE   Bujumbura   Victoria
Brazzaville   Mombasa
Cabinda   **Kinshasa**   Zanzibar
(Angola)   TANZANIA   **Dar es Salaam**
Luanda

1—BURUNDI
2—DJIBOUTI
3—EQUATORIAL GUINEA   ANGOLA   COMOROS
4—GAMBIA   **Moroni**
5—GUINEA-BISSAU   Mayotte I.
6—LESOTHO   (Fr.)
7—RWANDA   ZAMBIA   MAL.
8—SIERRA LEONE   **Lilongwe**
9—SWAZILAND   Lusaka   MADAGASCAR
10—TOGO   **Harare**
ZIMBABWE   MOZAMBIQUE   **Antananarivo**
LIB. —LIBERIA
MAL. —MALAWI
SEN. —SENEGAL   NAMIBIA
UGA. —UGANDA   (S.W. AFRICA)   BOTSWANA
U. VOL. —UPPER VOLTA
Fr.   —FRANCE   Walvis Bay   **Windhoek**
Port. —PORTUGAL   (S. Afr.)   **Gaborone**   **Pretoria**
S.Afr.—SOUTH AFRICA   Johannesburg   **Maputo**
Sp.   —SPAIN   **Mbabane**
SOUTH AFRICA   **Maseru** 6   Durban
Umtata

AFRICA (Political)

—— International boundaries
⚙ National capitals
● Other cities

0   800 mi.
0   1200 km

Cape Town   Port Elizabeth   INDIAN OCEAN

215

West longitude   East longitude

FIJI
Suva ✪

SOLOMON ISLANDS
Honiara ✪

VANUATU
Port-Vila ✪

New Caledonia (Fr.)

Norfolk I. (Aust.)

PACIFIC OCEAN

PAPUA NEW GUINEA
Bismarck Archipelago
New Britain (P.N.G.)
Port Moresby ✪

INDONESIA

Banda Sea

Arafura Sea

Timor Sea

Coral Sea

Great Barrier Reef

Torres Strait

Cape York Peninsula

Darwin ★

NORTHERN TERRITORY

Alice Springs
MacDonnell Ranges

Simpson Desert

Great Sandy Desert

Gibson Desert

WESTERN AUSTRALIA

Great Victorian Desert

Nullarbor Plain

Musgrave Ranges

SOUTH AUSTRALIA

Lake Eyre

AUSTRALIA

QUEENSLAND
Mount Isa

Townsville

Rockhampton

Toowoomba
Brisbane ★
Ipswich

GREAT DIVIDING RANGE

Darling River

Broken Hill

Newcastle
Sydney ★
Wollongong
Port Kembla
Canberra ✪
Bathurst
Wagga Wagga
Mt. Kosciusko (7,330 ft.; 2,230 m)

NEW SOUTH WALES

Murray River

VICTORIA
Bendigo
Ballarat
Geelong
Melbourne ★

Adelaide ★

Spencer Gulf
Port Augusta
Whyalla

Great Australian Bight

Kalgoorlie

Geraldton

Carnarvon
North West Cape

Perth ★

Albany

INDIAN OCEAN

Bass Strait

TASMANIA
Launceston
Hobart ★

Tasman Sea

NEW ZEALAND

NORTH ISLAND
North Cape
Whangarei
Auckland
Hamilton
Gisborne
Napier
Wellington ✪

Cook Strait

SOUTH ISLAND
Christchurch
Mt. Cook (12,349 ft., 3,760 m)
Dunedin
Invercargill

Tropic of Capricorn

West Longitude

GRAPH APPENDIX

THE EARTH: LAND AND WATER

THE EARTH: LAND AREA BY CONTINENTS

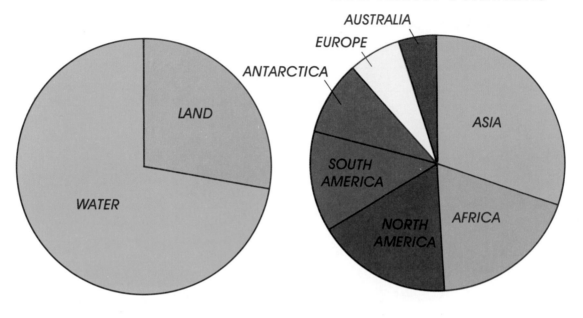

THE EARTH: LAND AREA BY COUNTRIES

THE UNITED STATES: LAND AREA BY STATES

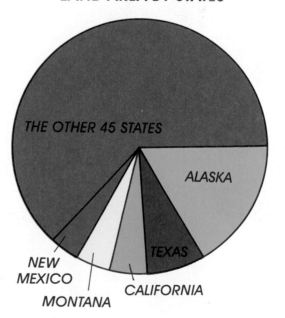

THE WORLD:
LARGEST COUNTRIES IN AREA

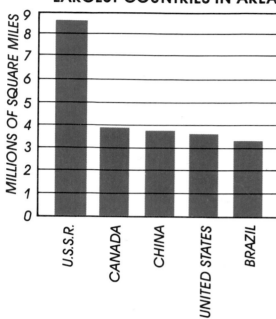

THE UNITED STATES:
LARGEST STATES IN AREA

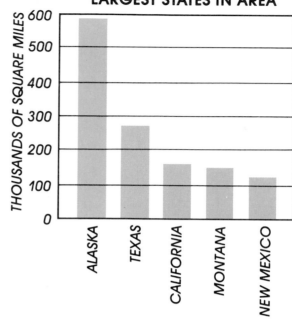

THE WORLD:
LARGEST ISLANDS IN AREA

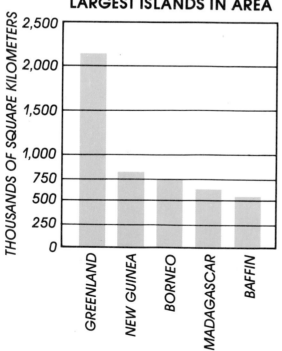

THE UNITED STATES:
LARGEST ISLANDS IN AREA

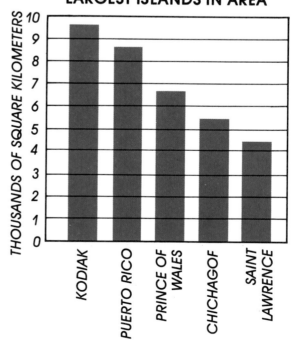

THE WORLD: LONGEST RIVERS

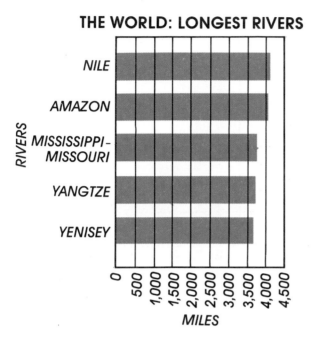

THE UNITED STATES: LONGEST RIVERS

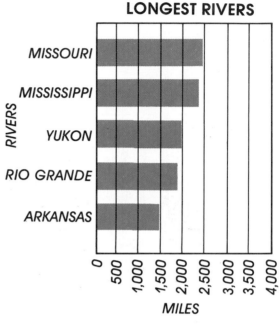

THE WORLD: LARGEST LAKES IN AREA

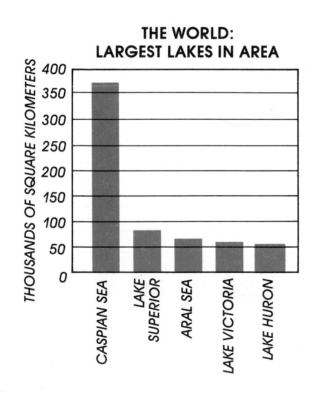

THE UNITED STATES: LARGEST LAKES IN AREA

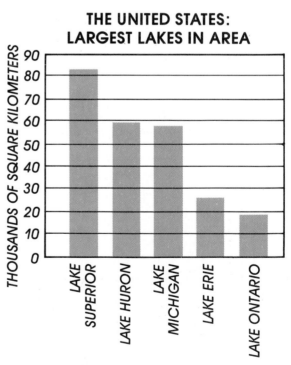

THE WORLD: LEADING PRODUCERS OF OIL

MILLIONS OF BARRELS

4,500 · 4,000 · 3,500 · 3,000 · 2,500 · 2,000 · 1,500 · 1,000 · 500 · 0

U.S.S.R. · SAUDI ARABIA · UNITED STATES · VENEZUELA · MEXICO

THE UNITED STATES: LEADING PRODUCERS OF OIL

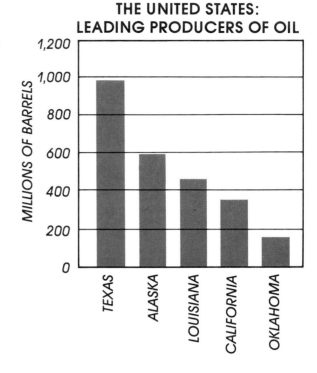

MILLIONS OF BARRELS

1,200 · 1,000 · 800 · 600 · 400 · 200 · 0

TEXAS · ALASKA · LOUISIANA · CALIFORNIA · OKLAHOMA

THE WORLD: LEADING PRODUCERS OF COAL

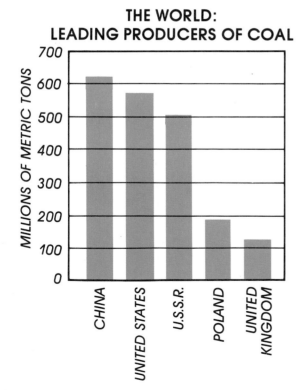

MILLIONS OF METRIC TONS

700 · 600 · 500 · 400 · 300 · 200 · 100 · 0

CHINA · UNITED STATES · U.S.S.R. · POLAND · UNITED KINGDOM

THE UNITED STATES: LEADING PRODUCERS OF COAL

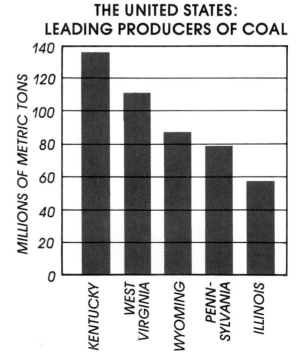

MILLIONS OF METRIC TONS

140 · 120 · 100 · 80 · 60 · 40 · 20 · 0

KENTUCKY · WEST VIRGINIA · WYOMING · PENN-SYLVANIA · ILLINOIS

220

THE WORLD: LEADING PRODUCERS OF WHEAT

MILLIONS OF SHORT TONS

125
100
75
50
25
0

U.S.S.R. — UNITED STATES — CHINA — INDIA — FRANCE

THE UNITED STATES: LEADING PRODUCERS OF WHEAT

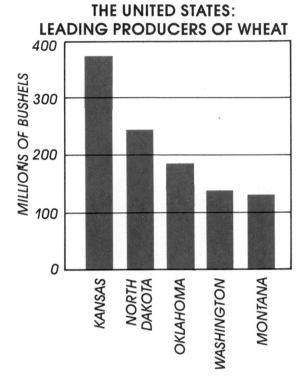

MILLIONS OF BUSHELS

400
300
200
100
0

KANSAS — NORTH DAKOTA — OKLAHOMA — WASHINGTON — MONTANA

THE WORLD: LEADING PRODUCERS OF FISH

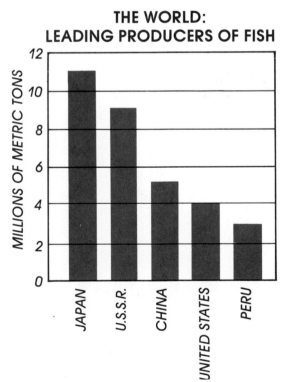

MILLIONS OF METRIC TONS

12
10
8
6
4
2
0

JAPAN — U.S.S.R. — CHINA — UNITED STATES — PERU

THE UNITED STATES: LEADING PRODUCERS OF FISH

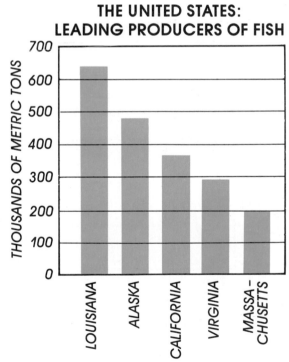

THOUSANDS OF METRIC TONS

700
600
500
400
300
200
100
0

LOUISIANA — ALASKA — CALIFORNIA — VIRGINIA — MASSA-CHUSETTS

AVERAGE MONTHLY TEMPERATURES: SAN FRANCISCO, CALIFORNIA

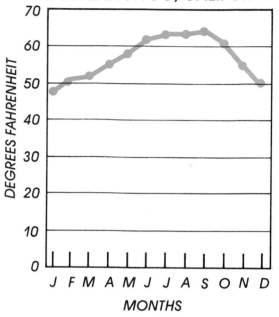

AVERAGE MONTHLY PRECIPITATION: SAN FRANCISCO, CALIFORNIA

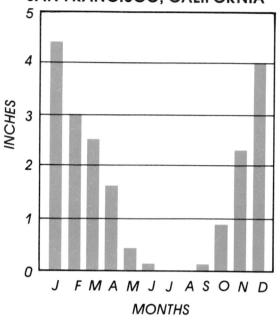

AVERAGE MONTHLY TEMPERATURES: WASHINGTON, D.C.

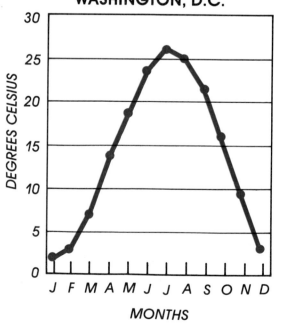

AVERAGE MONTHLY PRECIPITATION: WASHINGTON, D.C.

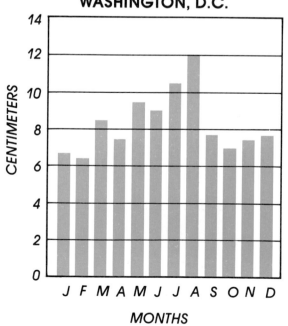

AVERAGE MONTHLY TEMPERATURES: MIAMI, FLORIDA

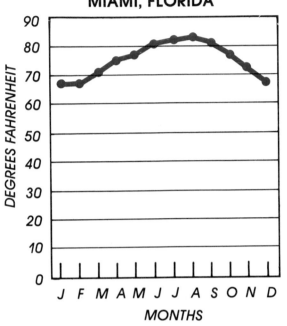

AVERAGE MONTHLY PRECIPITATION: MIAMI, FLORIDA

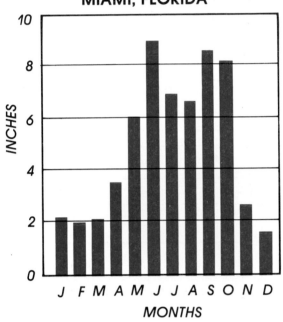

AVERAGE MONTHLY TEMPERATURES: CHICAGO, ILLINOIS

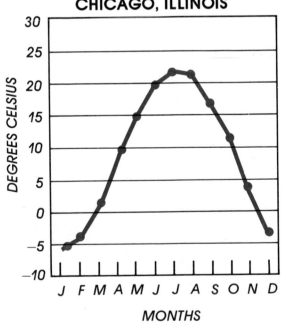

AVERAGE MONTHLY PRECIPITATION: CHICAGO, ILLINOIS

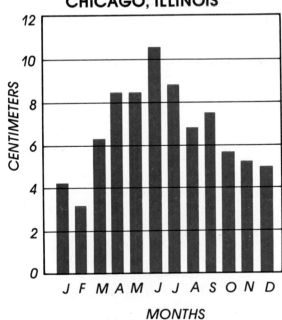

AVERAGE MONTHLY TEMPERATURES: NEW YORK, NEW YORK

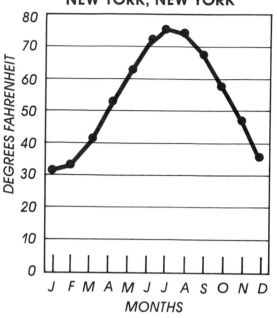

AVERAGE MONTHLY PRECIPITATION: NEW YORK, NEW YORK

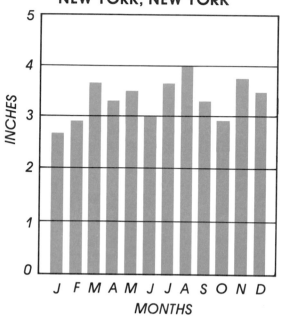

AVERAGE MONTHLY TEMPERATURES: HOUSTON, TEXAS

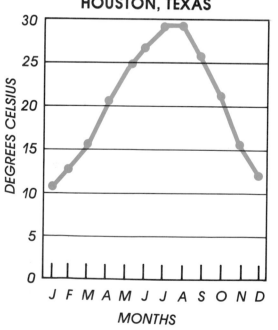

AVERAGE MONTHLY PRECIPITATION: HOUSTON, TEXAS

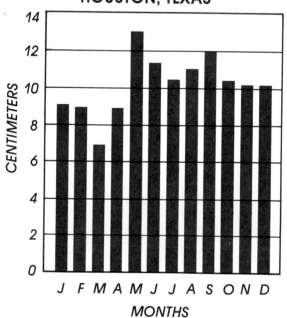

AVERAGE MONTHLY TEMPERATURES: MEXICO CITY, MEXICO

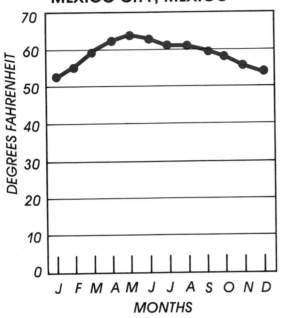

AVERAGE MONTHLY PRECIPITATION: MEXICO CITY, MEXICO

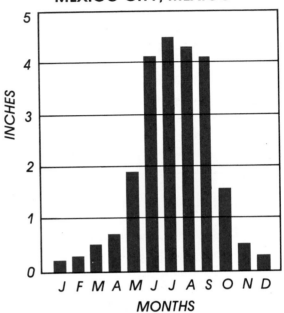

AVERAGE MONTHLY TEMPERATURES: SAN JUAN, PUERTO RICO

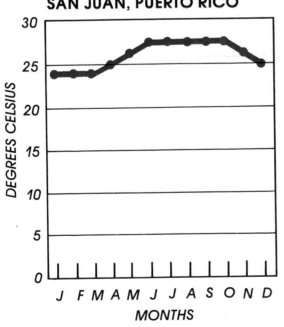

AVERAGE MONTHLY PRECIPITATION: SAN JUAN, PUERTO RICO

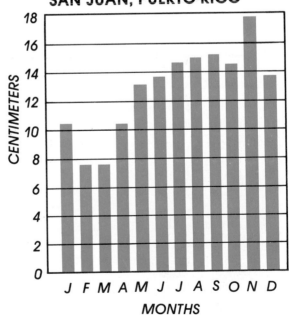

GAZETTEER

The Gazetteer is a geographical dictionary. It shows latitude and longitude for cities and certain other places. Latitude and longitude are shown in this form: 36°N/84°W. This means "36 degrees north latitude and 84 degrees west longitude." The page reference tells where each entry may be found on a map.

Africa. The earth's second largest continent. p. 19.

Alcoa (36°N/84°W). A community in eastern Tennessee. p. 39.

Antarctica. The earth's third smallest continent. p. 19.

Antarctic Circle. A line of latitude located at 66½° south latitude. p. 22.

Arctic Circle. A line of latitude located at 66½° north latitude. p. 22.

Arctic Ocean. The large body of salt water north of the Arctic Circle. p. 19.

Asia. The earth's largest continent. p. 19.

Atlanta (34°N/84°W). The capital of and most populated city in Georgia. p. 209.

Atlantic Ocean. The large body of salt water separating North America and South America from Europe and Africa. p. 19.

Austin (30°N/98°W). The capital of Texas. p. 208.

Australia. The smallest continent on the earth. p. 19.

Baton Rouge (30°N/91°W). The capital of Louisiana. Located on the Mississippi River. p. 17.

Bismarck (47°N/101°W). The capital of North Dakota. Located on the Missouri River. p. 16.

Bonneville Dam (46°N/122°W). Large dam on the Columbia River between Washington and Oregon. p. 208.

Cat Spring (30°N/96°W). A small community in Texas where the Salt Grass Trail Ride begins. p. 209.

Central America. The part of North America between Mexico and South America. p. 18.

Charleston (38°N/82°W). The capital of West Virginia. p. 17.

Chicago (42°N/88°W). A city located in Illinois, on the southern tip of Lake Michigan. One of six cities in the United States with a population of more than 1,000,000. p. 209.

Cincinnati (39°N/85°W). A large city in Ohio on the Ohio River. p. 209.

Columbia (34°N/81°W). The capital of South Carolina. Located on the Congaree River. p. 14.

Columbia River. A river that starts in the Rocky Mountains in Canada and flows into the Pacific Ocean along the Washington-Oregon boundary. p. 16.

Denver (40°N/105°W). The capital of and largest city in Colorado. Located at the base of the Rocky Mountains where they join the Great Plains. p. 16.

Detroit (42°N/83°W). The most populated city in Michigan. One of six cities in the United States with a population of more than 1,000,000. p. 209.

Eastern Hemisphere. The half of the earth east of the Prime Meridian. p. 21.

Equator. 0° line of latitude. A map line that circles the earth halfway between the two poles. p. 21.

Europe. The earth's second smallest continent. p. 19.

Great Plains. The large area of flat land in the United States that stretches from North Dakota to Texas. p. 16.

Greenwich. A place in London, England, located at 0° longitude. p. 22.

Gulf of Mexico. A body of salt water surrounded by the United States, Mexico, and Cuba. p. 18.

Hartford (42°N/73°W). The capital of Connecticut. Located on the Connecticut River. p. 17.

Houston (30°N/95°W). The most populated city in Texas. One of the six cities in the United States with a population of more than 1,000,000. Located near the Gulf of Mexico. p. 209.

Hudson River. A river that starts in mountains in the state of New York and flows south into the Atlantic Ocean at New York City. p. 40.

Humble (30°N/95°W). A small town in southeastern Texas. Located about 17 miles from Houston. Humble is a suburb of Houston. p. 200.

Lake Erie. The second smallest of the five Great Lakes. It borders on Canada, Michigan, Ohio, Pennsylvania, and New York. p. 17.

Lake Michigan. The third largest of the five Great Lakes. The only one of the Great Lakes located entirely in the United States. Its shores border on Michigan, Wisconsin, Illinois, and Indiana. p. 17.

Leningrad (60°N/30°E). The second most populated city in the Soviet Union. p. 27.

London (52°N/0° longitude). The capital and most populated city in the United Kingdom. Located along the Thames River. p. 27.

Los Angeles (34°N/118°W). One of six cities in the United States with a population of more than 1,000,000. Located in southern California along the Pacific coast. p. 208.

Manaus (3°S/60°W). A city in Brazil. Located on a branch of the Amazon River. p. 26.

Mexico City (19°N/99°W). The capital of Mexico. One of the most populated cities in the world. p. 210.

Miami (26°N/80°W). A large city in Florida located on the Atlantic Ocean. p. 209.

Miami Beach (26°N/80°W). A city in Florida located on the Atlantic Ocean. p. 209.

Minneapolis (45°N/93°W). The most populated city in Minnesota. Located on the Mississippi River. p. 209.

Morgan City (30°N/91°W). A small town in Louisiana near the Gulf of Mexico. p. 209.

Morris Township (41°N/74°W). A community in northern New Jersey. p. 41.

Morristown (41°N/74°W). A small community in northern New Jersey. p. 39.

Mount St. Helens (46°N/123°W). An active volcano that is located in Washington. p. 208.

Newark (41°N/74°W). The most populated city in New Jersey. p. 40.

New Orleans (30°N/90°W). The most populated city in Louisiana. One of the busiest ports in the United States. Located near the mouth of the Mississippi River. p. 209.

New York City (41°N/74°W). The most populated city in the United States. One of six cities in the country with a population of more than 1,000,000. Located in the state of New York at the mouth of the Hudson River. p. 209.

North America. The earth's third largest continent. p. 18.

Northern Hemisphere. The half of the earth that is north of the Equator. p. 21.

North Pole. The most northern place on the earth. p. 21.

Ohio River. A long river formed at Pittsburgh, Pennsylvania. Flows into the Mississippi River at Cairo, Illinois. p. 17.

Pacific Ocean. A large body of salt water off the west coast of the United States. The earth's largest ocean. p. 206.

Philadelphia (40°N/75°W). The most populated city in Pennsylvania. One of six cities in the United States with a population of more than 1,000,000. p. 209.

Phoenix (33°N/112°W). The capital of and most populated city in Arizona. p. 16.

Pittsburgh (40°N/80°W). The second most populated city in Pennsylvania. The most important steel center in the United States. p. 209.

Portland (46°N/123°W). The most populated city in Oregon. Located on the Willamette River. p. 208.

Potomac River. River on which Washington, D.C., is located. It also forms part of the boundary between Virginia and Maryland. p. 92.

Prime Meridian. 0° line of longitude that passes through Greenwich, England. It divides the earth into eastern and western hemispheres. p. 22.

Rocky Mountains. High mountains in the United States. They stretch from Canada to Mexico. p. 16.

St. Augustine (30°N/81°W). A city in Florida. It is the oldest city in the United States. p. 26.

San Antonio (30°N/98°W). A large city in Texas. Located on the San Antonio River. p. 208.

San Francisco (37°N/122°W). A large city in California. Located on San Francisco Bay, which is part of the Pacific Ocean. p. 208.

Scranton (41°N/76°W). A large coal-mining community located in northeastern Pennsylvania. p. 209.

South America. The earth's fourth largest continent. p. 19.

Southern Hemisphere. The half of the earth that is south of the Equator. p. 21.

South Pole. The most southern place on the earth. p. 21.

Tenochtitlán (19°N/99°W). City in Mexico first built by Aztecs. The city no longer exists, but Mexico City has grown at the same location. p. 70.

Tropic of Cancer. Line of latitude located at 23½° north latitude. p. 22.

Tropic of Capricorn. Line of latitude located at 23½° south latitude. p. 22.

Tucson (32°N/111°W). The second largest city in Arizona. p. 208.

Valley of Mexico. Low area in Mexico surrounded by mountains. Mexico City is located in this valley. p. 70.

Washington, D.C. (39°N/77°W). The capital of the United States. Located on the Potomac River. p. 17.

Western Hemisphere. The half of the earth west of the Prime Meridian. The hemisphere in which all of South America and North America is located. p. 21.

West Indies. A group of islands stretching from near Florida to near Venezuela. Part of North America. p. 18.

Wilmington (40°N/76°W). The most populated city in Delaware. p. 17.

GLOSSARY

The page references tell where each entry first appears in the text.

airport. A field where airplanes land and take off, including the buildings for keeping and repairing airplanes and taking care of passengers. p. 89.

Antarctic Circle. A line of latitude near the South Pole. p. 23.

antenna. A wire or a metal rod that picks up radio waves or signals. An antenna is used in radio and television communications. p. 191.

apartment. A single room or a group of rooms in which a person or a family lives. p. 76.

Arctic Circle. A line of latitude near the North Pole. p. 23.

area. The land for several miles around a community. p. 48.

assembly line. Group of people working together with the machines, tools, and parts needed to make a finished product, such as an automobile. p. 78.

astronaut. An American pilot or scientist who travels and works in space. p. 179.

auction. A public sale at which things are sold to the people who offer the most money for them. p. 138.

bar graph. A kind of graph that shows information by using bars. p. 32.

barbecue. Meat roasted over an open fire. p. 103.

bit. A cutting tool at the end of a drill. p. 148.

blacksmith. A person who works with iron and can fix tools and shoe horses. p. 107.

border. To be next to or to touch the edge of. Also, the line between two countries, states, or other places. p. 15.

business center. The part of a community in which most of the stores and offices are located. p. 83.

cable. A bundle of wires protected by a strong covering. p. 190.

cable car. A special form of transportation. A cable car runs on rails and is pulled by a steel cable moving under the street. p. 115.

cannery. A factory where fruit, vegetables, and other foods are canned. p. 132.

capital. A city where laws and plans for a state or a nation are made. p. 14.

Capitol. The building in Washington, D.C., where the men and women of Congress meet and work. p. 178.

car pool. A group of people who regularly ride together in a car to work or school. p. 113.

card catalog. An alphabetical listing of all books in a library. p. 170.

cargo ship. A large ship that carries different products as cargo. p. 91.

causeway. A raised road usually built across shallow water. p. 70.

census. A count of the number of people living in a nation. p. 29.

chamber of commerce. A group of business people who help their community. p. 48.

citizen. A person who is a member of a community, a state, or a country. p. 164.

citrus fruits. Fruits such as lemons, limes, oranges, and grapefruits, which grow on trees. p. 131.

climate. The kind of weather a place has all year. p. 74.

coal. A black rock that burns and makes energy. p. 142.

coastline. The edge of land that is next to an ocean or other body of water. p. 15.

combine. A machine that harvests wheat. It cuts the wheat, separates the grain from the stem and leaves of the plant, and cleans the grain. p. 130.

communication. The giving and receiving of information and ideas. p. 186.

community. A place where people live, work, and play. A community has houses, stores, places of worship, and other buildings. p. 12.

commuter. A person who travels regularly from the suburb to the city. p. 111.

compass rose. A drawing that shows where north, south, east, and west are on a map. Sometimes a compass rose is called a direction finder. p. 7.

Congress. The group of people who are elected to make laws for the United States. p. 156.

conservation. The care of natural resources so that they will not be spoiled and wasted but will be used wisely. p. 155.

continent. A large body of land on the earth. The continents are North America, South America, Asia, Africa, Europe, Australia, and Antarctica. p. 19.

corral. A fenced area in which horses and cattle are kept. p. 136.

council. A group of men and women who are chosen by the people in a community to make laws and plans for the community. p. 166.

creamery. A place where butter and other dairy products are made. p. 125.

crops. Plants that are grown in large amounts for food and other uses. p. 120.

dairy farm. A farm on which the main work is raising cows for milk, butter, and cheese. p. 123.

degree. A unit for measuring latitude and longitude. The symbol for degree is °. p. 22.

derrick. A steel tower over an oil well that holds the drilling machinery. p. 148.

dog guide. A dog that is specially trained to guide a blind person. p. 38.

east. The direction from which the sun seems to rise each morning. East is the opposite of west. When you face east, north is to your left and south is to your right. p. 4.

election. The choosing of a leader by voting. p. 167.

electricity. A form of energy that gives light and heat. p. 144.

Equator. A line drawn around the earth on maps and globes, halfway between the North Pole and the South Pole. The Equator divides the earth into the Northern Hemisphere and the Southern Hemisphere. p. 20.

factory. A building, or a group of buildings, in which machines and tools are used by workers to make products. p. 77.

fertilizer. Something put in soil to make crops grow better. p. 122.

fine. A certain amount of money paid as a punishment for not obeying a law. p. 167.

fish hatchery. A place for hatching fish eggs. Wildlife conservation people raise fish in a hatchery and then put them in a body of water. p. 159.

fuel. Anything that is burned to make heat or to make power for running machines. p. 144.

globe. A model of the earth. A globe shows how the earth looks from far away. p. 2.

goods. Things that are made, especially things made for sale. p. 80.

government. The leaders of a group who make the laws and see that the laws are carried out. The group may be all the people of a nation, state, county, city, or town. p. 166.

government city. A place where the leaders of a government meet to make laws and plans. p. 75.

grain elevator. A large building for storing grain. p. 130.

greenhouse. A building with a glass roof and glass sides that is kept warm for growing plants. p. 127.

Greenwich. A place in England through which the Prime Meridian passes. Half of all longitude lines are west of Greenwich. The other half are east of Greenwich. p. 23.

harvest. To gather crops from the land on which they grow. p. 122.

hay. Grass that is cut and dried and used as food for livestock. p. 125.

hemisphere. A half of the earth. p. 20.

housing development. A group of houses planned by a builder. The builder buys land and divides it into many lots on which houses are built. p. 100.

hurricane. A storm with very strong wind and, usually, very heavy rain. p. 150.

income. The money that a person earns. p. 120.

Independence Day. The birthday of the United States of America. People celebrate this holiday on July 4. p. 103.

interview. A meeting of people face-to-face to talk over a special subject. p. 59.

invent. To make something that no one else has ever made. p. 188.

irrigation. Carrying water through pipes, ditches, or canals to lands that are dry. p. 126.

island. A body of land with water all around it. p. 12.

judge. A person whose job is to hear and decide cases in a law court. Some judges are elected to the position. Other judges are named to the position. p. 167.

key. A special part of a map that explains the symbols on a map. p. 7.

lake. A body of water that has land all around it. p. 12.

latitude. An east-west line drawn on maps or globes. The Equator is a line of latitude. p. 22.

law. A rule that people must obey. p. 156.

line graph. A kind of graph that shows information by using lines. p. 33.

litter. Papers, cans, bottles, and other trash left lying about on the ground. p. 175.

livestock. Farm animals such as cows, horses, sheep, and pigs. p. 133.

lobster. A sea animal about 12 inches (31 cm) long with two big claws and eight legs. Lobsters are used for food. p. 154.

longitude. A north-south line drawn on maps or globes. The Prime Meridian is a line of longitude. p. 23.

magazine. A collection of stories and articles by different writers, usually printed every week or every month. p. 193.

map. A flat drawing that shows what the earth, or part of the earth, looks like. p. 6.

mayor. A community leader whose job is to help make the laws and to see that the laws are carried out. p. 166.

memorial. Something set up to help people remember a person or event. p. 178.

mineral. A substance found in the earth, such as coal, iron, and gold. A mineral is taken from the earth by mining. p. 142.

mining. Digging minerals from the earth. p. 142.

monument. Something set up to keep a person or an event from being forgotten. A monument may be a building, statue, arch, column, or tomb. p. 177.

mountain. Land that rises high above the land around it. p. 12.

museum. A building or rooms where people can see many interesting things on display. p. 43.

national forest. A forest that belongs to all the people of a country, or nation. National forests are cared for by the government of a nation. p. 157.

national park. A park that belongs to all the people of a country, or nation. National parks are cared for by the government of a nation. p. 42.

natural resource. Something useful to people and supplied by nature, such as land, water, forests, and minerals. p. 71.

newspaper. Sheets of paper printed every day or week, telling the news and having ads and other useful information. p. 193.

north. The direction toward the North Pole. North is the opposite of south. When you face the sun in the morning, north is to your left. p. 4.

North Pole. The most northern place on the earth. p. 4.

offshore oil platform. A large structure of either steel or concrete that is located in the ocean. The platform has equipment for drilling oil wells, as well as living space for workers and a helicopter landing deck. p. 148.

pasture. A field in which animals eat grass and other plants. p. 123.

penalty. A punishment, such as paying a fine or going to jail. p. 167.

peninsula. A piece of land that sticks out into the water. A peninsula has water almost all the way around it. Most of Florida is a peninsula. p. 15.

petroleum. An oily, dark liquid that is found in the earth. p. 147.

physical feature. A part of the earth. Rivers, lakes, seas, and mountains are examples of physical features. p. 15.

pictograph. A kind of graph that uses symbols instead of numbers. p. 30.

pie graph. A kind of graph drawn in the shape of a circle. Sometimes a pie graph is called a circle graph. p. 31.

pipeline. A system of pipes that carries certain substances, such as water or petroleum, over long distances. p. 151.

pollute. To spoil by adding something. For example, rivers, lakes, and oceans are polluted by dumping trash in them. p. 155.

port. A place where ships and boats load and unload products. p. 72.

Prime Meridian. The line of longitude from which other lines of longitude are measured. The Prime Meridian is numbered 0°. p. 23.

print. Words stamped in ink on paper. Print is an important means of communication. p. 193.

product. Something that people make or grow. p. 48.

property tax. A certain amount of money paid by people who own land, houses, and other buildings in a community. The amount of the tax depends on how much the property is worth. p. 173.

ranch. A large farm for raising cattle, sheep, or horses. p. 133.

ranger. A person whose job is to take care of national forests or national parks. p. 157.

recreation. Play, games, and sports. p. 171.

refinery. A factory with machines that change a natural resource to make it pure or to make different products from it. An oil refinery turns crude oil into gasoline, diesel oil, lubricating oil, and other useful products. p. 151.

reporter. A person who gathers the news for a newspaper. p. 194.

river. A long, narrow body of water that flows through the land toward a lake, sea, or ocean. p. 12.

rodeo. A series of contests that shows the skills of cowboys and cowgirls. p. 138.

rush hour. The time of day when most people are going to work or coming home from work. p. 111.

satellite. An artificial object that circles the planet earth carrying communications equipment. p. 190.

sawmill. A building where machines cut timber into boards of different sizes. p. 98.

scale. The size of a model, drawing, or map compared with what it stands for. On a map, scale shows distance. A scale of miles on a map tells how many miles on the earth one inch stands for. The scale used for a model or a drawing tells how big something is. p. 8.

sea. The ocean. Also, a very large body of salt water. p. 12.

The Seeing Eye. The oldest school that trains dogs to be guides for blind people. p. 53.

service. Work that helps other people, rather than work in which a product is made. p. 81.

solar energy. Power from the sun. p. 202.

soldier. A person who serves in an army. p. 36.

south. The direction toward the South Pole. South is the opposite of north. When you face the sun in the morning, south is to your right. p. 4.

South Pole. The most southern place on the earth. The South Pole is in Antarctica. p. 4.

state. A part of a country. There are 50 states in the United States. p. 14.

suburb. A community near a large city. p. 96.

subway. An electric train that travels underground. p. 93.

symbol. A drawing that stands for a real thing or place. On a map, a dot is a symbol for a city. p. 7.

table of contents. A part of a book or magazine that lists the names of chapters or articles and their pages. p. 195.

tanker. A large ship that carries oil or another liquid. p. 91.

tax. A certain amount of money that people pay to a community, state, or national government. Tax money is used to pay for many needed services in the community, state, or nation. p. 173.

taxicab. A special car. People pay the owner or driver of the car to drive them from place to place. p. 93.

temperature. Amount of heat or cold. p. 74.

time line. A scale drawing, standing for a period of time, on which dates are shown. A time line tells when things happened. p. 28.

trade. The buying and selling of products. p. 72.

traffic. The cars, trucks, buses, and people that move along a street or road. p. 111.

trail boss. A person in charge of a trail ride. p. 106.

trail ride. A trip on horseback along a planned route. p. 106.

transportation. The carrying of people and products from place to place. p. 71.

Tropic of Cancer. A line of latitude near the Equator in the Northern Hemisphere. p. 23.

Tropic of Capricorn. A line of latitude near the Equator in the Southern Hemisphere. p. 23.

valley. A lowland between hills or mountains. p. 68.

vote. A way of choosing a leader. p. 167.

weather. The way the air is at a certain time: sunny or cloudy, hot or cool, windy or calm, dry or wet. p. 74.

west. The direction in which the sun seems to set at night. West is the opposite of east. When you face west, north is to your right. South is to your left. p. 4.

wheat. A grasslike plant that bears grain, or seeds. Wheat is an important food crop. p. 88.

White House. The building in Washington, D.C., where the President of the United States lives and works. p. 177.

ZIP code. A group of numbers used when addressing mail to speed up mail delivery. p. 198.

AREA AND POPULATION OF THE FIFTY STATES

State	Area in sq mi	Area in sq km	Rank in area	Population (in thousands)	Rank in population
Alabama	51,609	133,667	29	3,917	22
Alaska	586,400	1,518,776	1	412	50
Arizona	113,909	295,024	6	2,794	29
Arkansas	53,104	137,539	27	2,296	33
California	158,693	411,015	3	24,196	1
Colorado	104,247	270,000	8	2,965	27
Connecticut	5,009	12,973	48	3,134	25
Delaware	2,057	5,328	49	598	47
Florida	58,560	151,670	22	10,183	7
Georgia	58,876	152,489	21	5,574	12
Hawaii	6,424	16,638	47	981	39
Idaho	83,557	213,822	13	959	40
Illinois	56,400	146,076	24	11,462	5
Indiana	36,291	93,994	38	5,468	13
Iowa	56,290	145,791	25	2,899	28
Kansas	82,264	213,064	14	2,383	32
Kentucky	40,395	104,623	37	3,662	23
Louisiana	48,523	125,675	31	4,308	18
Maine	33,215	86,027	39	1,133	38
Maryland	10,577	27,394	42	4,263	19
Massachusetts	8,257	21,386	45	5,773	11
Michigan	58,216	150,779	23	9,204	8
Minnesota	84,068	217,736	12	4,094	21
Mississippi	47,716	123,584	32	2,531	31
Missouri	69,686	180,487	19	4,941	15
Montana	147,138	381,087	4	793	44
Nebraska	77,227	200,018	15	1,577	35
Nevada	110,540	286,299	7	845	43
New Hampshire	9,304	24,097	44	936	42
New Jersey	7,836	20,295	46	7,404	9
New Mexico	121,666	315,115	5	1,328	37
New York	49,576	128,402	30	17,602	2
North Carolina	52,719	136,542	28	5,953	10
North Dakota	70,665	183,022	17	658	46
Ohio	41,222	106,765	35	10,781	6
Oklahoma	69,919	181,090	18	3,100	26
Oregon	96,981	251,181	10	2,651	30
Pennsylvania	45,333	117,412	33	11,871	4
Rhode Island	1,214	3,144	50	953	41
South Carolina	31,055	80,432	40	3,167	24
South Dakota	77,047	199,552	16	686	45
Tennessee	42,244	109,412	34	4,612	17
Texas	267,339	692,408	2	14,766	3
Utah	84,916	219,932	11	1,518	36
Vermont	9,609	24,887	43	516	48
Virginia	40,815	105,711	36	5,430	14
Washington	68,192	176,617	20	4,217	20
West Virginia	24,181	62,629	41	1,952	34
Wisconsin	56,154	145,439	26	4,742	16
Wyoming	97,914	253,597	9	492	49

INDEX

Key to Pronunciation

a	hat, cap	i	it, pin	ou	house, out	zh	measure, seizure
ā	age, face	ī	ice, five	sh	she, rush	ə	represents:
ã	care, air	ng	long, bring	th	thin, both		a in about
ä	father, far	o	hot, rock	ŦH	then, smooth		e in taken
ch	child, much	ō	open, go	u	cup, butter		i in pencil
e	let, best	ô	order, all	ù	full, put		o in lemon
ē	equal, see	oi	oil, voice	ü	rule, move		u in circus
ėr	term, learn						

The Key to Pronunciation above is reprinted from *The World Book Dictionary*. © 1981 by permission of J. G. Ferguson Publishing Company, Chicago, IL 60601.

A

Africa, 19, 20
Airplanes and airports, 87, 89 – 90, 100, 127
Alaska, 15, 152
Antarctic Circle, 23
Antarctica, 19, 20
Antenna, radio, 191
Apartment buildings, 76 – 77, 100
Arctic Circle, 23
Arctic Ocean, 15
Arizona, 126
Asia, 19, 20
Assembly line, 78 – 79
Astronauts, 179
Atlanta, Georgia, 74 – 75, 157 – 158
Atlantic Ocean, 15, 190
Auctions, livestock, 138
Australia, 19, 20
Automobiles. *See* Cars.
Aztec Indians, 68, 70

B

Barbecues, 103
Bay Area Rapid Transit (BART), 114
Bell, Alexander Graham, 188
Blacksmith, 107
Books, 195
Buses, 87, 111, 115
Business center, of city, 83

C

Cable cars, 115
Cable, telephone, 190
California, 15, 123, 126
Canada, 19
Cannery, 132
Capital(s)
    of states, 14, 175
    of United States, 75, 175 – 181
Capitol, 178
Car pools, 113

Cargo ships, 91
Cars
    making of, 78 – 79
    as transportation, 87, 111 – 114
Cattle, 133 – 136
Causeways, 70
Census, 29
Central America, 19
Chamber of commerce, 48 – 49
Chicago, Illinois, 85
Chinook Indians, 158 – 159
Cincinnati, Ohio, 71 – 72
Cities
    and commuter transportation,
        111 – 114
    growth of, 68 – 75, 142
    homes in, 76 – 77
    recreation in, 82 – 86
    transportation for, 87 – 93, 115
    working in, 77 – 81
    See also the name of the individual
        city.

Citrus farms, 131 – 132
Climate, 74
Coal mining, 142 – 146
Coastline, 15
Colorado, 15
Columbia River, 158 – 159
Combine (machine), 130
Communication, 186 – 187
    by letter, 196 – 201
    print, 193 – 196
    radio, 191
    telephone, 188 – 190
    television, 192
Communities, 12 – 13
    laws for, 164 – 166

recreation in, 59 – 61, 82 – 86,
    105 – 110
services provided in, 168 – 173
studying, 36 – 63
working in, 48 – 52, 100 – 101
    See also Cities; Suburbs; Towns.
Commuting, 111 – 115
Compass rose, 7
Congress, 156 – 157, 178
Connecticut, 15
Conservation, of resources, 155 – 159
Continents, 19
Copper, 142
Corral, 136
Council, town or city, 166
Cows, dairy, 123 – 125
Creamery, 125
Crops, 120
    See also Farming.

D
Dairy farms, 123 – 125
Dams, 159
Degrees, of latitude and longitude, 22
Delaware, 15
Denver, Colorado, 73
Derricks, oil, 148, 150
Detroit, Michigan, 78
Directions, 4, 7
Dog guides, 38, 53 – 58

E
Earth, 2
Eastern Hemisphere, 20
Elections, 167
Electricity, 142 – 144
Equator, 20
Europe, 19, 20, 190

F

Factories, 77—79
Farming
  citrus, 131—132
  dairy, 123—125
  long ago and today, 120—122
  vegetable, 126—128
  wheat, 129—130
Fertilizer, 122
Fines, 167
Firefighters, 101
Fishing, 153—154
Florida, 15, 74, 126, 131
Ford Mansion, 42—45
Forests. *See* National forests.
Fort Nonsense, 42, 46
Fuel, 144, 147

G

Gasoline, 111—113, 147
  See also Oil.
Globe, 2, 4
Gold, 73, 142
Goods, 80
Government, 166, 175
Government city, 75, 175—181
Grain elevators, 130
Graphs, 29—33, 141
Great Plains, 15, 73, 129
Greenhouse, 127—128
Greenwich, England, 23
Gulf of Mexico, 149—150

H

Harvesting, 122, 130, 132
Hatcheries, fish, 159
Hawaii, 15, 133

Hay, 125, 134
Hemispheres, 20—21
Homes, 76—77, 100
Housing developments, 100
Houston, Texas, 96, 98—99, 100, 101,
    106, 109—110, 111, 138—139, 174,
    198—199
Hudson River, 158
Humble, Texas, 96—101, 103—106, 199,
    201
Hurricane, 150

I

Income, 120
Independence Day, 103
Inventions, 188—192
Iowa, 133
Iron, 142
Irrigation, 126
Island, 12, 15

J

Jefferson, Thomas, 178
Jockey Hollow, 42, 46—47
Judge, 167

K

Kansas, 129, 133
Kennedy, John F., 180

L

Lake, 12
Lake Erie, 158
Latitude, 22—23, 25—27
Laws, 156, 164—166, 175
Leaders, 166—167, 175, 176
Letters, 196—201
Library services, 170

Litter, 175
Livestock, 133 – 138
Lobsters, 154
Longitude, 23, 25 – 27
Los Angeles, California, 84 – 85, 101

M
Machines
  in coal mining, 146
  farm, 122, 130
Magazines, 194 – 195
Maine, 154
Map
  of a community, 13
  of earth's continents, 19
  of Eastern Hemisphere, 21
  key, 7
  of Morris County, New Jersey, 41
  of Morristown and Morris
    Township, New Jersey, 41
  of Morristown National Historical
    Park, 44
  of a neighborhood, 117
  of New Jersey, 40
  of North America, 18
  of Northern Hemisphere, 21
  from a photograph, 7
  reading, 6 – 11
  scale, 8 – 11
  of a school, 11
  showing directions, 4
  showing latitude and longitude lines,
    22, 24, 26 – 27
  of South Carolina, 14
  of Southern Hemisphere, 21
  symbols, 7
  of Texas postal ZIP code areas, 200

  of United States, 16 – 17, 39
  of United States coalfields, 145
  of United States oil fields, 149
  of United States postal ZIP code
    regions, 199
  of Valley of Mexico, 70
  of Washington Metropolitan Area
    Transit System, 92
  of Western Hemisphere, 21
Marconi, Guglielmo, 191
Maryland, 176
Mayor, 166
Mexico, 19
Miami, Florida, 82
Miami Beach, Florida, 74
Mining, coal, 142 – 146
Morgan City, Louisiana, 149
Morristown and Morris Township,
  New Jersey, 36 – 61, 112 – 113
Morristown National Historical Park,
  42 – 47
Mountains, 12, 15
Museums, 43, 45

N
National forests, 157
National parks, 42 – 47, 157
Natural resources. *See* Resources,
  natural.
Nebraska, 15, 133
New Jersey, 15, 40
  See also Morristown and Morris
    Township, New Jersey.
New York, 123, 127
New York City, 86
Newspapers, 193 – 194
North America, 18 – 19, 20

North Pole, 4, 23
Northern Hemisphere, 20

O
Offshore oil platforms, 148 – 150
Ohio River, 72
Oil, 98 – 99, 147 – 152
Oklahoma, 133
Oranges, 131 – 132
Oregon, 158 – 159

P
Pacific Ocean, 15, 190
Parks
    community, 59 – 61, 171
    national, 42 – 47, 157
Pastures, 123
Penalty, 167
Peninsula, 15
Pennsylvania, 123, 144 – 145
Petroleum. *See* Oil.
Physical features, of earth, 15
Pipelines, oil, 151 – 152
Pittsburgh, Pennsylvania, 157 – 158
Police, 167
Pollution, 155, 157 – 158
Ports, 72
Postal service, 196 – 201
Potomac River, 180, 181
President of United States, 176, 177
Prime Meridian, 23
Print communication, 193 – 196
Products, company, 48, 50

R
Radio, 191
Railroads and trains, 74, 87, 88 – 89, 127

Ranching, 133 – 137
Rangers, forest, 157
Recreation, 59 – 61, 82 – 86, 105 – 110, 171
Refineries, oil, 151
Reporter, newspaper, 194
Resources, natural, 142, 147
    conservation of, 112, 155 – 159
    and growth of towns and cities, 71, 73, 98 – 99
    See also Coal mining; Gasoline; Gold; Oil.
Revolutionary War, 44 – 47
Rhode Island, 15
Rivers, 12
Road repair, 169
Rodeos, 138 – 139
Roosevelt, Theodore, 156 – 157
Rules. *See* Laws.
Rush hour, 111

S
Salmon, 158 – 159
San Antonio, Texas, 83
San Francisco, California, 114 – 115
Satellites, 190
Saudi Arabia, 152
Sawmills, 98
Scale, map, 8 – 11
Scranton, Pennsylvania, 145
Sea, 12
Seeing Eye, 53 – 58
Services, of communities, 81, 168 – 173
Ships, 87, 91
Silver Burdett Company, 51 – 52
Solar energy, 202

South America, 19, 20
South Carolina, 15
South Pole, 4, 23
Southern Hemisphere, 20
States, 14 – 17, 175
    See also the name of the individual state.
Suburbs, 96, 99, 100, 111 – 115
Subways, 92 – 93, 114
Symbols, map, 7

T
Tankers, oil, 91
Taxes, 173
Taxicab, 93, 111, 115
Telephone, 188 – 190
Television, 192
Temperature, 74
Tenochtitlán, 68 – 71
Texas, 15, 126, 133
    See also Houston, Texas; Humble, Texas.
Time line, 28
Towns, 96 – 110
    See also Communities; Suburbs.
Trade, 72
Traffic problems, 111
Trail boss, 106
Trail ride, 106 – 110
Trains. *See* Railroads and trains.
Trans-Alaska Pipeline, 152
Transportation, 186
    for cities, 87 – 93, 115
    and growth of cities, 71 – 72, 74 – 75
    from suburbs to cities, 111 – 114

Tropic of Cancer, 23
Tropic of Capricorn, 23
Trucks, 87, 89, 111, 125, 127, 128

U
United States
    farming in, 120 – 136
    maps of, 16 – 17, 39, 145, 149, 199
    and natural resources, 142 – 154
    population of, 29

V
Valley of Mexico, 68 – 70
Vegetable farms, 126 – 128
Virginia, 180
Voting, 167

W
Washington, D.C., 75, 92, 175 – 181
Washington, George, 36, 42, 45 – 47, 176, 181
Washington, state of, 158 – 159
Weather, 74
West Indies, 19
Western Hemisphere, 20
Wheat farms, 129 – 130
White House, 177
Wisconsin, 123
Work and workers, 77 – 81, 100 – 101

Z
ZIP code, 198 – 201
Zoo, 172

CREDITS

Cover: Gregory Hergert
Unit openers: Gregory Hergert
Graphs and charts: Joe LeMonnier/Craven
Design Studio, Inc.
Maps: R.R. Donnelley Cartographic Services

3 4 5 6 7 8 9 10—RRD—88 87 86 85 84